ACPL ITEM
DISCARDED

Rowe, Fred A.
The career connection

YO-AAV-839

The
Career
Connection

A Guide to College Majors and Their Related Careers

by Fred A. Rowe, Ed. D.

REVISED EDITION

Allen County Public Library
Ft. Wayne, Indiana

The Career Connection — *A Guide to College Majors and Their Related Careers*

©1991, JIST Works, Inc.

All rights reserved. No part of this book may be reproduced in any form or by any means, or stored in a data base or retrieval system, without prior permission of the publisher except in case of brief quotations embodied in critical articles or reviews.

JIST Works, Inc.
720 North Park Avenue
Indianapolis, IN 46202-3431
1-317-264-3720 • Fax: 1-317-264-3709

The Career Connection II: Another book by Dr. Rowe that uses a similar format to this book but is for those considering technical majors. Price: $13.95, ISBN: 0-942784-83-9.

Other Titles: JIST publishes a variety of career reference, trade (bookstore style) books on job seeking and career information.
Order Information: See the last page of this book for an order form or contact us for additional information. Qualified Schools and institutions may request our catalog of over 500 career related books, videos and software.

Errors and omissions: We have been careful to provide accurate information throughout this book. But it is possible that errors have been inadvertently introduced. Please consider this in making any career plans or other important decisions. Trust your own judgment above all else and in all things.

Library of Congress Cataloging-In-Publication Data
Rowe, Fred A.
    The Career Connection : a guide to college majors
and their related careers / by Fred A. Rowe. -- Rev. ed.
        p. cm.
    Includes index.
    ISBN 0-942784-82-0 : $15.95
    1. College graduates--Vocational guidance--United States--
Directories.   2. United States--Occupations--Directories.
3. Vocational qualifications--United States--Directories.
I. Title.
HF5382.5.U5R68   1991   91-22629
331.7'023--dc20   CIP

ISBN: 0-942784-82-0

Preface

Because selecting a career is so vital, nearly everyone needs help with it. Most career decisions are made on the informal advice of friends, relatives, or others yet recent research indicates that decisions made on this basis are less satisfactory than those based on qualified career guidance.

The Career Connection is a career counseling tool designed to assist a person explore career alternatives that require technical training or education. By presenting all major technical education programs and their related jobs, it allows the reader to quickly identify training or education options and their related careers and requirements. This approach makes it very easy to use and an effective initial counseling tool.

How to Use This Book

The book has been designed to be flexible by providing several ways to approach the career exploration process. You can use the table of contents to quickly identify a college major, then turn to that section in the book for more detailed information. You can also look up a specific job title in the Career Index and its related educational requirements. Regardless of the starting point, *The Career Connection* provides:

1. A general description of each educational major, and the type of career-related work it leads to.
2. Various job titles, outlook for future openings and starting salaries related to each major.
3. A code number for each occupation that cross-references the reader to the *Dictionary of Occupational Titles*, a major career information source published by the U.S. Department of Labor.
4. The types of courses typically required in each area of study.
5. High school courses that best prepare for the area of study or that indicate an ability to succeed in that area.

One of the unique features of this book is its listing of specific courses typically required in each field of study. This approach allows you to relate your previous interests and school abilities to the requirements of a specific area of study. Many people find this information particularly helpful in making a decision. The information on typical starting salaries and the outlook for job openings are also important factors to consider in career planning.

This variety of information is provided in a simple-to-use format that should be useful for most users. This book provides information that is general in nature and can't replace the careful review of a college's catalog of course offerings and requirements. Many colleges will have specific requirements that may differ some from those presented here and the names of their major areas of study may also differ. But the information contained here will be helpful in identifying areas of interest that are worthy of more consideration.

About the Author

Fred A. Rowe holds a doctorate degree from Arizona State University. He has been a secondary school counselor for eight years. He functioned as assistant dean of Admissions and Financial Aids for Brigham Young University for 13 years where he administered School Relations, Admissions, Financial Aids, and a nationally award-winning alumni advising network. He currently is coordinator of the Counselor Education Program and director of the Career Assessment Center at Brigham Young University. He consults with various national and state organizations that deal with developing state models for comprehensive counseling and guidance programs, creating programs that deal with assisting displaced workers and homemakers with educational and career assessment and advisement, and enhancing the transition from high school to community colleges and universities.

Table of Contents

College Majors Described in this Book

Appendices

Additional information to help you get the most from this book.

Indices

A listing of all the occupations that are listed in this book cross-referenced in various ways.

Introduction

Make this book work for you. Its format is simple. The information is easy to use, without unnecessary details.

The first part of *The Career Connection* is a self-study guide describing the educational majors and related occupations in alphabetical order. Simply use the table of contents to look up areas of interest.

The second part of *The Career Connection* contains the appendices and indices. Several of these will be particularly helpful if you don't yet have a career objective. You will find brief descriptions of each below.

THE APPENDICES

Appendix A—INTERPRETING THE *Dictionary of Occupational Titles*. A major source of career information.

Appendix B —EDUCATIONAL ALTERNATIVES. This section will acquaint you with a variety of educational choices and some terms you will need to understand for college.

Appendix C—YOUR INTEREST AREAS. This section outlines 26 career clusters and will ask you to identify the ones you find interesting and will also identify relevant pages in *The Career Connection* that relate to each cluster.

Appendix D—PERSONAL SUMMARIES. This section asks you to summarize your ideas after you have had a chance to explore the information in this book.

Appendix E—TAKING THE NEXT STEPS. This section identifies specific tasks that will be important for you as you start the process of getting into college.

THE INDICES

Index of Courses. Lists high school courses and cross-references you to related college majors.

Index of Majors. An alphabetical listing of the college majors described in this book and their related page numbers.

Index of Careers. Lists career areas in alphabetical order and cross-references the related college majors required for entry.

Use the appendices to help you plan your career and education. If you are still in high school, a resource that you will want to use is your high school counselor. If you have been out of high school for some time, an effective resource for you will be located on the campus of the college or colleges you are considering. You will be smart to contact the admissions and financial aids offices for more information on getting into college. Most schools also offer the services of an educational advisement office and career counseling. These areas can be most helpful in identifying the specific requirements for each major at that school. Remember, the information in this book is general in nature. Each major's offerings will be unique.

Sources of Information

The information contained in this book was assembled from a variety of sources. They include survey information from selected school placement offices; information from national professional organizations; and various government sources. Some of the governmental data sources include: "Federal Civilian Workforce Statistics: Occupations of Federal White Collar and Blue-Collar Workers," published by the U.S. Office of Personnel Management; "Comparison of Annual Salaries in Private Industry with Salary Rates of Federal Employees," published by the U.S. Department of Labor as well as other DOL sources.

I hope you enjoy using the book and that you find it helpful.

DR. FRED ROWE

COLLEGE MAJORS

ACCOUNTING

Tremendous job opportunities are available to accounting majors in management, public, or government accounting. Management accountants provide information and advice as a member of the management team in the planning and direction of the company's operations. The public accountant offers auditing, tax works, and other financial advice services. The Internal Revenue Service, United States Accounting Office, and local and state government agencies provide employment opportunities in government accounting. Employment opportunities continue to increase throughout the United States and in many foreign countries with CPA firms, governments, and industries.

COURSE REQUIREMENTS

Accounting
Auditing
Business Law
Business Mathematics
Business Policy
Computer Science
Economic

Finance
Marketing
Marketing
Organizational Behavior
Systems

OPTIONS WITHIN MAJOR

Financial Auditing
Management Accounting

Management Accounting
Taxation

RECOMMENDED HIGH SCHOOL COURSES

Business Education
English

Math (3 years)
Science

CAREERS	D.O.T. NUMBER	OUTLOOK	AVERAGE INITIAL SALARY
Bachelor Degrees			
Accountant	160.167-010	Good/Exc.	$22,000
Auditor	160.162-014	Good/Exc.	25,000
Bank Examiner	160.167-046	Fair	21,000
Budget & Forecast Accountant	160.167-014	Good/Exc.	25,000
Controller	168.117-014	Fair	25,000
Cost Accountant	160.167-018	Good/Exc.	22,000
General Accountant	160.167-010	Excellent	19,000
Property Accountant	160.167-022	Good	19,000
Revenue Agent	160.167-050	Good	19,000
Securities Trader	162.157-042	Excellent	25,000
Systems & Procedures Accountant	160.167-02	Excellent	22,000
Tax Accountant	160.162-010	Excellent	23,000
Graduate Degrees			
Auditor	160.162-014	Excellent	29,000
Bursur	160.167-042	Good	28,000
Professor	090.227-010	Good	28,000
Tax Specialist	160.167-038	Excellent	27,000

ADVERTISING

Advertising exists to sell products and services in the marketplace by communicating with the American consumer, who is the best served user of goods in the world today. It also performs an institutional function—keeping business such as airlines or banks in the public eye; reminding consumers about what services are available to them. Employment opportunities may be found in advertising agencies, department stores, media, public relations, professional and trade associations.

COURSE REQUIREMENTS

Advertising, Copy
Advertising Principles
Advertising Strategy
Art
Journalism
Layout Campaigns
Marketing Principles
Media Design

Media Sales Problems
Persuasion Process
Photo Journalism
Pictoral Photography
Production
Promotion Management
Retail

OPTIONS WITHIN MAJOR

Business Administration
Design

Journalism
Marketing

RECOMMENDED HIGH SCHOOL COURSES

Art
English (4 years)
History
Journalism

Literature
Speech
Typing

CAREERS	D.O.T. NUMBER	OUTLOOK	AVERAGE INITIAL SALARY
Bachelor Degrees			
Account Executive	164.167-010	Good	$26,000
Advertising Manager	164.117-010	Good	23,000
Commercial Artist	141.061-022	Fair	15,000
Copy Artist	131.167-014	Fair	15,000
Promotion Manager	163.117-018	Good	22,000
Graduate Degree			
Professor	090.227-010	Fair	26,000

AEROSPACE AND AERONAUTICAL ENGINEERING

This area of study produces graduates whose specialized skills are in high demand. The purpose of aerospace engineering is to develop aerospace vehicles. It includes knowledge from many areas such as electrical and chemical engineering, design, structure, and analysis of materials. A high number of graduates move into military service as engineering officers; many others find employment in the aerospace industry.

COURSE REQUIREMENTS

Aerodynamics
Aeroelasticity
Aerospace Materials
Aerothermochemistry
High Speed Aerodynamics
Numerical Methods
Numerical Simulation

Propulsion
Space Technology
Structural Dynamics
Superaerodynamics
Vehicle Design
Viscous Fluids

OPTIONS WITHIN MAJOR

Aerodynamics
Design

Propulsion
Testing

RECOMMENDED HIGH SCHOOL COURSES

Chemistry
English

Math (3 years)
Physics

CAREERS	D.O.T. NUMBER	OUTLOOK	AVERAGE INITIAL SALARY
Bachelor Degrees			
Aerodynamicist	002.061-010	Good/Exc.	$29,000
Aeronautical Design Engineer	002.061-022	Excellent	29,000
Aeronautical Engineer	002.061-014	Excellent	30,000
Design Engineer	002.061-026	Excellent	27,000
Stress Analyst	002.061-030	Good/Exc.	26,000
Test Engineer	002.061-018	Good	23,000
Graduate Degrees			
Aeronautical Engineer	002.061-014	Excellent	34,000
Professor	090.227-010	Good	31,000
Research Engineer	002.061-026	Excellent	36,000

AFRICAN STUDIES

African Studies is an interdisciplinary program typically referred to as "Area Studies." It integrates ideas and principles from anthropology, literature, history, geography, and economics. This broadly based education allows one to do historical research, social, political, and economic analysis, and literary criticism. Students often continue on to advanced studies in law, business administration, and liberal arts, or may become involved in teaching or government service.

COURSE REQUIREMENTS

Africa and Early Man
African Art
African Roots in America
Archaeology of Africa
Central Africa
Colonization of Africa
Cultural Anthropology
Cultures of Africa
East Africa
Economics of Africa

Folklore Medicine
Geography of Africa
Inter-African Relations
Mediterranean Africa
Political Thought
Racial Issues
Social Anthropology
South Africa
Uncommon Languages
Wildlife of Africa

OPTIONS WITHIN MAJOR

Anthropology
Geography

Political Science

RECOMMENDED HIGH SCHOOL COURSES

Art
Economics
English
Foreign Language

Geography
History
Literature

CAREERS	D.O.T. NUMBER	OUTLOOK	AVERAGE INITIAL SALARY
Bachelor Degrees			
Biographer	052.067-010	Fair/Poor	Varies
Correspondent	131.267-018	Fair	$23,000
Foreign Service Officer	188.117-106	Fair	22,000
Historian	052.067-022	Fair/Poor	21,000
Import/Export Agent	184.117-022	Good	22,000
Intelligence Expert	059.267-010	Good	24,000
Public Relations Specialist	165.067-010	Fair	25,000
Publications Editor	132.037-026	Poor	20,000
Travel Agent	225.157-010	Good	12,000
Graduate Degrees			
Foreign Service	051.067-010	Good	27,000
Professor	090.227-010	Good	27,000
Researcher	052.167-010	Good	25,000

AGRICULTURAL ECONOMICS

Agricultural economics and agri-business management are a synthesis of training in economics, scientific agriculture, business management, accounting, and finance. Graduates find employment opportunities in farm and ranch management, banking, transportation, food processing, farm equipment and products, real estate, food retailing, and other related agri-business firms. Both governmental agencies and private firms have need of graduates in this major who are able to work on the improvement of agricultural products, marketing, and distribution.

COURSE REQUIREMENTS

Accounting and Finance
Agri-business Finance
Agri-business Mgt. Economics
Agricultural Marketing
Agronomy-Horticultur
Animal Science
Computer Science
Demand and Price Analysis
Economics and Agriculture

Farm & Ranch Management
Food Science
Futures Trading
Land and Range Economics
Mathematics and Statistics
Micro/Macro-Economics Theory
Public Policy
Real Estate Appraisal & Finance
Research Methods

OPTIONS WITHIN MAJOR

Agri-business
Agricultural Economics
Farm-Ranch Management

Food Industries Management
Real Estate

RECOMMENDED HIGH SCHOOL COURSES

Accounting
Agriculture
Botany
Business/Economics

Chemistry
Math
Vocational Agriculture

CAREERS	D.O.T. NUMBER	OUTLOOK	AVERAGE INITIAL SALARY
Associate Degrees			
Agri-business Technologist		Fair	$18,000
Agricultural Supplier		Good	16,000
Farm Manager		Fair	20,000
Farm Real Estate Salesman	186.117-058	Fair	20,000
Food Processing Agent		Good	14,000
Food Retailer Distributor		Fair	16,000
Bachelor Degrees			
Agricultural Agent	096.127-010	Fair	23,000
Agricultural Appraiser	188.167-010	Good/Exc.	21,000
Claims Adjustor	191.117-046	Fair	19,000
Extension Service Agent	096.127-014	Good	25,000
Farm Management Adviser	096.127-018	Fair	22,000
Market Research Analyst		Good/Exc.	23,000
Rural Bank Manager	186.117-038	Good/Exc.	20,000
Vocational Agricultural Teacher	091.227-010	Fair	18,000
Graduate Degrees			
Agri-business Management		Good/Exc.	23,000
Agricultural Financier	050.067-010	Good/Fair	24,000
Agricultural Policy Adviser	096.127-010	Good	26,000
Market/Data Analyst	050.067-010	Good	23,000
Professor	090.227-010	Good	25,000

AGRONOMY

Agronomists are scientists who face the challenge of solving man's most critical world problem: providing enough food for mankind. Basic principles of the biological and physical sciences are applied to the management of soils and the production of food, fiber, and ornamental plants by the agronomist. Private industry and government agencies provide a good job market.

COURSE REQUIREMENTS

Animal Science
Botany
Chemistry
College Algebra
Crop Ecology
Crop Science
Field Crop Production

Irrigated Soils
Nursery Science
Pest Management
Soil Fertility
Soil Science
Water Resources

OPTIONS WITHIN MAJOR

Agri-business
Management Advisory Services

Production

RECOMMENDED HIGH SCHOOL COURSES

Botany
Business
Chemistry

English
Math
Vocational Agriculture

CAREERS	D.O.T. NUMBER	OUTLOOK	AVERAGE INITIAL SALARY
Associate Degree			
Salesman	227.357-010	Good	$18,000
Bachelor Degrees			
Agricultural Agent	096.127-010	Fair	23,000
Agricultural Engineer	013.061-010	Fair	27,000
Agronomist	040.061-010	Good	19,000
Land/Water Use Analyst	029.081-010	Good	20,000
Range Manager	040.061-046	Fair	15,000
Soil Scientist	040.061-058	Good	20,000
Soil/Water Conservationalist	040.061-054	Good	20,000
Teacher	091.227-010	Fair/Good	18,000
Graduate Degrees			
Professor	090.227-010	Good	25,000
Researcher		Good	27,000

AMERICAN STUDIES

0American Studies is an interdisciplinary program typically referred to as "Area Studies." It integrates ideas and principles from anthropology, literature, history, geography, and economics. This broadly based education allows one to do historical research, social, political, and economic analysis, and literary criticism. Students often continue on to advanced studies in law, business administration, and liberal arts or may become involved in teaching or government service.

COURSE REQUIREMENTS

American Architecture
American Art
American Family History
American Novel
American Political Thought
Archeology
Canada-American Relations
Cultures of North America
Ecology
Economic History of North America
Economic Thought

Economics of Energy and Environment
Folklife and Folklore
Geography of North America
Hispanic Southwest
Inter-American Relations
Modern American Language Usage
Motion Pictures in America
Native Peoples of North America
Themes in American Literature
Urban Government

OPTIONS WITHIN MAJOR

Business
Culture

Economics
Politics

RECOMMENDED HIGH SCHOOL COURSES

Art
Economics
English
Foreign Language

Geography
History
Literature

CAREERS	D.O.T. NUMBER	OUTLOOK	AVERAGE INITIAL SALARY
Bachelor Degrees			
Biographer	052.067-010	Fair/Poor	Varies
Correspondent	131.267-018	Fair	$23,000
Foreign Service Officer	188.117-106	Fair	22,000
Historian	052.067-022	Fair/Poor	21,000
Import/Export Agent	184.117-022	Good	22,000
Intelligence Expert	059.267-010	Good	24,000
Public Relations Specialist	165.067-010	Fair	25,000
Publications Editor	132.037-026	Poor	20,000
Travel Agent	225.157-010	Good	14,000
Graduate Degrees			
Foreign Service	051.067-010	Good	27,000
Professor	090.227-010	Good	27,000
Researcher	052.167-010	Good	25,000

ANIMAL SCIENCE

0Animal science provides a combination of classroom teaching, laboratory studies, and practical experience in the study of animals that serve mankind, Graduates develop skills applying to: the production and management of meat, dairy, and food industries; meat packing and production; practical livestock farming and management; swine, poultry, beef, dairy, or sheep operations; consulting and field work; and preveterinary medicine. Although a majority of the graduates become self-employed, others seek employment with government agencies, pharmaceutical companies, civil agencies, or colleges and universities (teaching and research).

COURSE REQUIREMENTS

Accounting
Agricultural Economics
Agronomy
Animal Anatomy
Animal Breeding
Animal Hygiene
Animal Physiology and Anatomy
Animal Physiology
Applied Animal Nutrition
Chemistry

Feeds and Feeding
Horse Production
Horticulture
Livestock Evaluation
Math
Meat Processing
Milk and Milk Products
Poultry Production
Veterinary Pharmacology

OPTIONS WITHIN MAJOR

Business and Industry
Preveterinary

Production
Science

RECOMMENDED HIGH SCHOOL COURSES

Agriculture
Algebra
Biology
Chemistry

English (3 years)
Geometry
Vocational Agriculture

CAREERS	D.O.T. NUMBER	OUTLOOK	AVERAGE INITIAL SALARY
Associate Degrees			
Cattle Rancher	410.161-018	Fair	$17,000
Dairy Manager	040.061-018	Fair	17,000
Federal Meat Grader		Fair	15,000
Food & Meat Inspector	316.684-018	Fair	16,000
Poultry Manager	040.061-018	Fair	16,000
Bachelor Degrees			
Dairy Technologist	040.061-022	Good	23,000
Livestock Extension Agent		Fair/Good	25,000
Graduate Degrees			
Animal Scientist	040.061-014	Good	28,000
Dairy Scientist	040.061-018	Fair	27,000
Geneticist	041.061-050	Good	20,000
Poultry Scientist	040.061-042	Fair	25,000
Professor	090.227-010	Good	25,000
Research & Development	040.061-042	Good	27,000

ANTHROPOLOGY

0Anthropologists study the world's varied peoples and their cultures. They want to know how and why the variety arose. They also seek the similarities we all share—our human nature. Social and cultural anthropologists study living peoples in all aspects of their lives—economic and technological, social, political, aesthetic, religious, etc. The former specialists emphasize the importance of social arrangements as determiners of differences and similarities. The cultural anthropologists emphasize culture, consisting of the customary thinking and feeling patterns with the world and themselves. Archaeologists are mainly the anthropologists of the peoples no longer living; they excavate and interpret earlier cultures and societies from their material remains. Linguistic, biological and psychological anthropologists specialize in particular bodies of information and certain methods, but all of them are still concerned with differences. The breadth of this subject makes it exceptionally valuable as liberal education preparation for a profession or for life, however, graduate work to at least the master level is important in securing most employment in the field.

COURSE REQUIREMENTS

Ancient Cultures
Archaeological Methods
Biological Anthropology
Economic Institutions
Field Archaeology
Human Osteology
Intercultural Communications

Moral and Ritual Institutions
Museology
Old World Civilization
Psychological Anthropology
Social Anthropology
Theory of Archaeology

OPTIONS WITHIN MAJOR

Applied Anthropology
Archaeology

Museology

RECOMMENDED HIGH SCHOOL COURSES

English (4 years)
Geography
History

Humanities
Literature

CAREERS	D.O.T. NUMBER	OUTLOOK	AVERAGE INITIAL SALARY
Bachelor Degrees			
Archaeological Technician		Fair	$15,000
Museum Technician	102.381-010	Fair	15,000
Graduate Degrees			
Anthropologist	055.067-010	Fair	24,000
Applied Anthropologist		Fair	23,000
Archaeologist	056.067-018	Good	23,000
Archivist	101.167-010	Good	24,000
Consultant/Researcher		Fair	24,000
Cultural Anthropologist	055.067-010	Fair	24,000
Ethnologist	055.067-022	Good	23,000
Linguist	059.067-014	Fair/Good	22,000
Museum Curator	102.017-010	Fair/Good	25,000
Physical or Social Anthropologist	055.067-014	Fair	25,000
Professor	090.227-010	Fair	27,000

ARCHITECTURE

Architects provide a wide variety of professional services to individuals, organizations, corporations, or government agencies planning a building project. Architects are involved in all phases of development of a building project, from the initial discussion of general ideas through construction. Their duties require a variety of skills — design, engineering, managerial, and supervisory.

Most architects work for architectural firms, builders, real estate firms, or other business that have large construction programs. Some work for government agencies responsible for housing, planning, or community development. Employment opportunities are also found in the Federal Government, mainly for the Departments of Defense, Interior, Housing and Urban Development, and the General Services Administration.

COURSE REQUIREMENTS

Architectural History
Architectural Theory
Calculus
Design
Economics
Engineering & Urban Planning
English

Fine Arts
Geometry
Graphics
Physics
Structural Elements
Urban Design

OPTIONS WITHIN MAJOR

Architecture

Urban Planning

RECOMMENDED HIGH SCHOOL COURSES

Biology
Drawing
English
General Science

Geometry
Mechanical Drawing
Public Speaking

CAREERS	D.O.T. NUMBER	OUTLOOK	AVERAGE INITIAL SALARY
Bachelor Degrees			
Architect	001.061-010	Good	$25,000
Drafter	001.261-010	Excellent	17,000
Marine Architect	001.061-014	Fair	22,000
Urban Planner	199.167-014	Good	22,000
Graduate Degrees			
Architect	001.061-010	Good/Exc.	30,000
Professor	090.227-010	Good	27,000

ART

Art and design prepares creative leaders in the visual arts who are sensitive to the aesthetic needs of society. An appreciation for the arts and their importance in the role of the total development of the individual is emphasized. Graduates combine the artistic elements with manufacturing techniques to find employment in industry and economy. Increased leisure time in our society has increased the interest in arts and crafts, and several graduates are able to set up successful studies in ceramics, crafts, painting, printmaking, and sculpting. Despite the competition in some areas, graduates are also successful in obtaining jobs in education.

COURSE REQUIREMENTS

American Art
Art History
Business Practices
Ceramics
Contemporary Art
Drawing
Greek Art
Hand Lettering

Medieval Art
Philosophy of Fine Arts
Print Making
Recreational Arts and Crafts
Sculpture
Survey of Architecture
Water Color

OPTIONS WITHIN MAJOR

Art Education
Art History
Ceramics
Drawing

Painting
Print making
Sculpture
Studio Art

RECOMMENDED HIGH SCHOOL COURSES

Art

Design

CAREERS	D.O.T. NUMBER	OUTLOOK	AVERAGE INITIAL SALARY
Bachelor Degrees			
Advertising Designer	247.387-018	Good	$16,000
Art Therapist	076.127-014	Fair	17,000
Audio Visual			
Production Specialist	149.061-010	Good	17,000
Cartoonist	141.061-010	Fair	14,000
Fashion Artist	141.061-014	Good	17,000
Furniture Designer	142.061-022	Fair	15,000
Illustrator	141.061-022	Good	17,000
Layout Designer	141.061-018	Good	16,000
Medical Illustrator	141.061-026	Good	22,000
Quick Sketch Artist	149.041-010	Fair	12,000
Sculptor	144.061-018	Fair	Varies
Set Designer	142.061-046	Fair	17,000
Studio Artist	141.061-010	Fair	Varies
Teacher (Elementary)			
(Secondary)	149.021-010	Good	18,000
Graduate Degrees			
Art Director	141.061-018	Fair	44,000
Professor	090.227-010	Good	25,000

ASIAN STUDIES

Asian Studies is an interdisciplinary program typically referred to as "Area Studies." It integrates ideas and principles from anthropology, literature, history, geography, and economics. This broadly based education allows one to do historical research, social, political and economic analysis, and literary criticism. Students often continue on to advanced studies in law, business administration, and liberal arts, or may become involved in teaching or government service.

COURSE REQUIREMENTS

Asian and International Politics
Asian Culture
Asian Literature
Asian Political Thought
Asian Religions and Thought
Business and Culture
Chinese Law
Chinese Literature
Economic Development
History of Asia
Humanities in Asia

International Business
International Trade and Finance
Japanese Law
Japanese Literature
Korean Law
Korean Literature
Modern Asia
Oriental Art and Architecture
Oriental Mythology
Social Sciences in Asia

OPTIONS WITHIN MAJOR

Business
Economics
Government

Philosophy
Politics

RECOMMENDED HIGH SCHOOL COURSES

Art
Economics
English
Foreign Language

Geography
History
Literature

CAREERS	D.O.T. NUMBER	OUTLOOK	AVERAGE INITIAL SALARY
Bachelor Degrees			
Biographer	052.067-010	Fair/Poor	Varies
Correspondent	131.267-018	Fair	$23,000
Foreign Service Officer	188.117-106	Fair	22,000
Historian	052.067-022	Fair/Poor	21,000
Import/Export Agent	184.117-022	Good	22,000
Intelligence Expert	059.267-010	Good	24,000
Public Relations Specialist	165.067-010	Fair	25,000
Publications Editor	132.037-026	Poor	20,000
Travel Agent	225.157-010	Good	14,000
Graduate Degrees			
Foreign Service	051.067-010	Good	27,000
Professor	090.227-010	Good	27,000
Researcher	052.167-010	Good	25,000

BOTANY

Agricultural and ecological problems in the world will be solved, in part, by those with in-depth knowledge of botany. Development of plant hybrids that are disease resistant and produce a high plant yield will be a fundamental part of world prosperity and cultural mobility. Botany offers professional training in a wide variety of careers including governmental services, research institutions, and industry.

COURSE REQUIREMENTS

Animal Science
Biochemistry
Biology
Botany
Chemistry
Ecology
Genetics
Math

Microbiology
Plant Anatomy
Plant Classification
Plant Cytology
Plant Geography
Plant Pathology
Plant Physiology

OPTIONS WITHIN MAJOR

Disease Control
Farming Research
Forestry

Genetics
Governmental Agencies
Range Science

RECOMMENDED HIGH SCHOOL COURSES

Biology
Botany
Chemistry

English
Math (3 years)

CAREERS	D.O.T. NUMBER	OUTLOOK	AVERAGE INITIAL SALARY
Bachelor Degrees			
Botanist	041.061-038	Fair/Poor	$22,000
Plant Breeder	041.061-082	Fair	20,000
Graduate Degrees			
Geneticist	041.061-050	Good	20,000
Nematologist	041.061-066	Fair	22,000
Plant Cytologist	041.061-042	Good	24,000
Plant Pathologist	041.061-086	Good	27,000

BUSINESS EDUCATION

Business education teachers are qualified to teach office skills, business economics, bookkeeping, and related office or clerical subjects. Related to office education is socio-business and distributive education where students are instructed in sales, promotion, buying operations, market research communications, and management. Many business education majors are qualified for work in the business community as well as teaching in secondary schools. Vocational programs are expanding across the nation, and the employment prospects for business teachers should remain positive.

COURSE REQUIREMENTS

Business Communications
Business Law
Business Policy
Computer Science
Economics
Elementary Accounting

Financial Management
General College Math
Marketing Management
Operations Management
Statistics

OPTIONS WITHIN MAJOR

Business
Distributive Education

Office Education

RECOMMENDED HIGH SCHOOL COURSES

Business
English (4 years)

Math (3 years)
Typing

CAREERS	D.O.T. NUMBER	OUTLOOK	AVERAGE INITIAL SALARY
Bachelor Degrees			
Administrative Assistant	185.117-167	Excellent	$17,000
Office Manager	185.117-167	Good/Exc.	19,000
Teacher	091.227-010	Good/Exc.	18,000
Graduate Degrees			
Business Administrator	185.117-167	Good	35,000
Professor	090.227-010	Good	25,000

BUSINESS MANAGEMENT

Business management programs are designed to prepare students for responsible leadership in their chosen profession by providing in-depth training and experience in marketing, production, finance, individual and group behavior, and other management skills. Occupational opportunities for graduates in this field remain positive throughout the country both in government and private industry. Besides preparing for management and administration of business, many students go on to study law or Master of Business Administration programs.

COURSE REQUIREMENTS

Accounting
Business Computing
Business Mathematics
Business Policy
Buying Behavior
Commercial Law
Financial Management
General College Math
Investments
Macro Economics

Marketing
Micro Economics
Operations Analysis
Operations Management
Organizational Behavior
Public Policy
Real Estate
Retailing
Risk Management
Statistics

OPTIONS WITHIN MAJOR

General Business
Finance
Marketing

Operating/Systems Analysis
Retailing

RECOMMENDED HIGH SCHOOL COURSES

English (4 years)
General Science

Math (3 years)

CAREERS	D.O.T. NUMBER	OUTLOOK	AVERAGE INITIAL SALARY
Bachelor Degrees			
Banker	160.167-000	Good	$24,000
Broker	162.157-014	Good	30,000
Budget/Management Analyst	160.207-010	Good/Exc.	20,000
Buyer	162.157-018	Fair/Good	22,000
Credit Manager	186.167-022	Good/Exc.	18,000
IRS Agent		Good	20,000
Job Analyst	166.267-018	Good/Exc.	19,000
Labor Relations Manager	166.167-034	Fair	35,000
Market Research Analyst	050.067-014	Good/Exc.	24,000
Personnel Manager	166.117-018	Excellent	30,000
Placement Director	166.167-014	Good	27,000
Purchasing Agent	162.157-038	Good	24,000
Retail Management	185.117-167	Good/Exc.	22,000
Sales Manager	163.167-018	Good	23,000
Stock Broker	251.157-010	Good	31,000
Systems Analyst	012.167-066	Good/Exc.	25,000
Graduate Degrees			
Airport Manager	184.117-026	Fair	29,000
Director of Public Service	184.117-010	Fair	25,000
Director of Transportation	184.117-010	Fair	24,000
Management Analyst	161.167-010	Excellent	29,000
Marketing Research Analyst	050.067-014	Excellent	29,000
Professor	090.227-010	Good	29,000

CANADIAN STUDIES

Canadian Studies is an interdisciplinary program typically referred to as "Area Studies." It integrates ideas and principles from anthropology, literature, history, geography, and economics. This broadly based education allows one to do historical research, social, political, and economic analysis, and literary criticism. Students often continue on to advanced studies in law, business administration, and liberal arts, or may become involved in teaching or government service.

COURSE REQUIREMENTS

American Architecture
American Art
Archaeology of North America
Canadian Educational System
Canadian Foreign Policy
Canadian Political Issues
Canadian Political Thought
Canadian Society
Canada-United States Relations

Cultures of Canada
Ecology
Economic History of North America
Economic Thought
Folklife and Folklore
Geography of North America
International Business
International Communications
Native Peoples of North America

OPTIONS WITHIN MAJOR

Business
Economics

Politics

RECOMMENDED HIGH SCHOOL COURSES

Art
Economics
English
Foreign Language

Geography
History
Literature

CAREERS	D.O.T. NUMBER	OUTLOOK	AVERAGE INITIAL SALARY
Bachelor Degrees			
Biographer	052.067-010	Fair/Poor	Varies
Correspondent	131.267-018	Fair	$23,000
Foreign Service Officer	188.117-106	Fair	22,000
Historian	052.067-022	Fair/Poor	21,000
Import/Export Agent	184.117-022	Good	22,000
Intelligence Expert	059.267-010	Good	24,000
Public Relations Specialist	165.067-010	Fair	25,000
Publications Editor	132.037-026	Poor	20,000
Travel Agent	225.157-010	Good	14,000
Graduate Degrees			
Foreign Service	051.067-010	Good	27,000
Professor	090.227-010	Good	27,000
Researcher	052.167-010	Good	25,000

CHEMICAL ENGINEERING

The chemical engineers' principal activity is changing raw materials into useful and valuable products, and as such they are widely employed applying these principles of chemical research and engineering to production and processing operations. Virtually all qualified graduates find employment in some form of research, design, operation, or management, especially as it deals with current problems such as energy or pollution. The chemical engineering technician assists the chemical engineer in all industries by obtaining and analyzing data, operating equipment, and planning and carrying out experiments. Most technicians find employment in areas such as industrial design, environmental engineering, and related research and developmental projects.

COURSE REQUIREMENTS

Analytical Geometry
Applied Ordinary Differential
Equations
Calculus
Chemical Engineering
Chemical Engineering Kinetics
Chemical Engineering
Thermodynamics
Chemical Process Principles
Elements of Electrical Engineering

Engineering Mechanics-Statics
Fundamentals of Physics
Organic Chemistry
Physical Chemistry
Plant Design & Economics
Principles of Chemistry
Process Synthesis
Science of Engineering Metals
Unit Operations

OPTIONS WITHIN MAJOR

Bioengineering
Energy and Environment
Management

Nuclear Engineering
Research
Semiconductor Fabrication

RECOMMENDED HIGH SCHOOL COURSES

Chemistry
Drafting
Industrial Shop

Math (3 years)
Physics

CAREERS	D.O.T. NUMBER	OUTLOOK	AVERAGE INITIAL SALARY
Associate Degrees			
Chemical Engineer			
Technician	008.261-010	Good/Exc.	$19,000
Chemical Operator	558.585-014	Good	20,000
Laboratory Tester	022.281-018	Good	18,000
Bachelor Degrees			
Chemical Design Engineer	008.061-014	Good	28,000
Chemical Engineer	008.061-018	Excellent	30,000
Chemical Equipment			
Engineer	008.151-010	Good	26,000
Chemical Operator	558.585-014	Good	24,000
Environmental Scientist	029.081-010	Excellent	23,000
Nuclear Engineer	015.061-014	Excellent	27,000
Graduate Degrees			
Biomedical Engineer	019.061-010	Excellent	35,000
Engineer	008.061-018	Fair/Good	35,000
Petroleum Engineer	010.061-018	Good/Exc.	33,000
Professor	090.227-010	Fair/Good	29,000
Researcher	008.061-022	Good/Exc.	35,000

CHEMISTRY

Chemistry is the study of matter and the manner in which it changes and reacts as well as the laws governing those reactions. Chemists develop and simplify models and theories and perform research in biochemistry, geochemistry, organic chemistry, analytical chemistry, inorganic chemistry, and physical chemistry. Employment opportunities in chemistry are excellent. Qualified, creative graduates find employment teaching or performing research in virtually any industry.

COURSE REQUIREMENTS

Analytical Chemistry
Analytical Geometry
Biochemistry
Biophysical Chemistry
Calculus
Chemical Literature
Chemistry
Computer Programming
Inorganic Chemistry
Instrumental Analysis

Organic Compounds
Organic Chemistry
Physical Chemistry
Physics
Physiological Chemistry
Principles of Chemistry
Principles of Physics
Qualitative Analysis
Quantitative Analysis
Scientific Computing

OPTIONS WITHIN MAJOR

Analytical Chemistry
Biochemistry
Inorganic Chemistry

Organic Chemistry
Physical Chemistry

RECOMMENDED HIGH SCHOOL COURSES

Chemistry
English (4 years)

Math (all available courses)
Physics

CAREERS	D.O.T. NUMBER	OUTLOOK	AVERAGE INITIAL SALARY
Associate Degrees			
Chemical Lab Technician	022.261-011	Good	$18,000
Chemical Operator	558.585-014	Good	17,000
Laboratory Tester	022.281-018	Good	16,000
Bachelor Degrees			
Assayer	022.281-010	Fair	20,000
Chemical Laboratory Chief	022.161-014		23,000
Chemical Operator	558.585-014	Good	24,000
Chemical Technologist	078.261-010	Good/Exc.	23,000
Chemist	022.061-010	Excellent	25,000
Criminologist	029.281-010	Fair	20,000
Science Writer	131.267-026	Good	24,000
Soil Scientist	040.061-058	Good	20,000
Teacher	091.227-010	Fair	18,000
Graduate Degrees			
Biochemist	041.061-026	Good	25,000
Production Chemist		Excellent	24,000
Professor	090.227-010	Fair	28,000
Research Chemist		Excellent	36,000

CHINESE

The study of chinese literature and language prepares graduates with a cultural understanding of and ability to communicate with people in Asian lands. Increased international commerce, research, and interaction have created a need for people well-trained in Chinese language, literature, and thought. Apart from practical language applications in government and literary work, several graduates find teaching opportunities on the college level.

COURSE REQUIREMENTS

Chinese   Grammar
Composition   Literature
Conversation   Phonetics
Cultural Civilization   Translation

OPTIONS WITHIN MAJOR

Business   Translation
Education

RECOMMENDED HIGH SCHOOL COURSES

Foreign Language   Humanities
Geography   Literature
History

CAREERS	D.O.T. NUMBER	OUTLOOK	AVERAGE INITIAL SALARY
Bachelor Degrees			
Customs Official	168.267-022	Fair	$16,000
Foreign Service Officer	188.117-106	Fair	22,000
Import/Export Agent	184.117-022	Good	22,000
Intelligence Expert	059.267-010	Good	24,000
Interpreter	137.267-010	Fair/Good	19,000
Language Researcher	059.067-014	Fair	22,000
Public Relations Specialist	165.067-010	Fair	25,000
Scientific Writer		Fair	24,000
Teacher	019.227-010	Poor	18,000
Translator	137.267-018	Good	19,000
Travel Agent	225.157-010	Good	12,000
Graduate Degrees			
Professor	090.227-010	Good	25,000
Scientific Linguist	059.067-014	Fair	24,000

CIVIL ENGINEERING

Combining a knowledge of mathematics, chemistry and physics, the civil engineer develops means to utilize the materials and forces of nature in: the design and construction of structures; pollution control; and other engineering endeavors. The civil engineering technician assists the engineer in providing facilities and structures for the community, industry, and government. A shortage of civil engineers and the need for solutions to technical problems (waste disposal, mass transportation, urban growth) will continue to increase job possibilities for civil engineering graduates.

COURSE REQUIREMENTS

Analytical Geometry
Calculus
Civil Engineering Design
Elementary Soil Mechanics
Elements of Electrical Engineering
Engineering Graphics
Engineering Mechanics-Dynamics
Engineering Mechanics-Statics
Engineering Seminar
Engineering Surveying
Geology for Engineers
Highway Engineering

Hydraulic Engineering
Hydraulics and Fluid Flow History
Hydrology
Introduction to Civil Engineering
Microbiology
Principles of Physics
Professional, Legal, & Economic
Problems in Engineering
Properties of Materials
Structural Steel/Reinforced
Concrete Design
Structural Theory

OPTIONS WITHIN MAJOR

Environmental Engineering
Geotechnical Engineering
Highway & Transportation

Solid Mechanics
Water Resources
Engineering

RECOMMENDED HIGH SCHOOL COURSES

Algebra
Calculus
Chemistry

Geometry
Physics

CAREERS	D.O.T. NUMBER	OUTLOOK	AVERAGE INITIAL SALARY
Associate Degree			
Civil Engineering Tech.	005.061-014	Good/Exc.	$19,000
Bachelor Degrees			
Airport Engineer	005.061-010	Good	27,000
Civil Engineer	005.061-014	Good/Exc.	29,000
Construction Engineer	005.061-034	Excellent	23,000
Highway Engineer	005.167-022	Good	21,000
Hydraulic Engineer	005.061-018	Good	27,000
Irrigation Engineer	005.061-022	Fair/Poor	21,000
Sanitation Engineer	005.061-030	Good/Exc.	27,000
Structural Engineer	005.061-034	Excellent	25,000
Teacher	091.227-010	Fair/Good	18,000
Transportation Engineer	005.061-038	Good	27,000
Graduate Degrees			
Professor	090.227-010	Good	29,000
Research & Development		Good	31,000

CLASSICAL LANGUAGES

The multitude of languages in the western world are often related to the original classical languages, Greek and Latin. Study of these languages is essential for Biblical and Early Christian studies, romance philosophy, or studies of ancient history and comparative literature. Many students contemplating graduate work in linguistics or the professional school of law, medicine, and dentistry find the classical languages an advantageous undergraduate study. Teaching positions are available in Latin, but Greek is essentially used on the collegiate level.

COURSE REQUIREMENTS

Classical Greek Culture
Grammar and Composition
Greek and Latin Masterpieces
  in English Translation
Greek and Roman Mythology
  in English Translation
Greek Drama in English
Translation
Greek Reading/Composition

Latin
Latin Culture
Latin Literature
Latin Stylistic/Literary
Analysis
Masterpieces of Greek
Literature
Masterpieces of Latin
Literature

OPTIONS WITHIN MAJOR

Classical Civilization
Greek

Latin

RECOMMENDED HIGH SCHOOL COURSES

Humanities
Language

Literature

CAREERS	D.O.T. NUMBER	OUTLOOK	AVERAGE INITIAL SALARY
Bachelor Degrees			
Archivist	101.167-010	Fair	$23,000
Genealogist	052.067-018	Poor/Fair	17,000
Intelligence Specialist	059.267-010	Fair/Good	24,000
Research Assistant	109.267-010	Fair/Good	19,000
Teacher	091.227-010	Fair	18,000
Translator	137.267-018	Fair/Good	19,000
Graduate Degrees			
Archaeologist	055.067-018	Good	23,000
Anthropologist	055.067-010	Fair	24,000
Historian	052.067-022	Fair/Poor	Varies
Professor	090.227-010	Fair	25,000
Scientific Linguist	059.067-014	Fair	23,000

CLOTHING AND TEXTILES

Clothing and textiles deals with the wise selection, effective use, and proper care of clothes in order to meet the needs of individuals and to provide training in the textile and apparel industries. Careers are open in demonstration work, designing, dressmaking, fashion illustration, merchandising, promotion, purchasing, manufacturing, textile testing, and theatrical costuming. Graduate work is also available for those interested in college teaching, research, or extension services. Employment opportunities are usually available in metropolitan areas with large department stores or other large clothing and textile firms.

COURSE REQUIREMENTS

Apparel Design
Apparel Evaluation
Children's Clothing
Clothing Construction
Clothing and Human Behavior
Clothing Merchandising
Dress and Pattern
Economy: Society, and Public
Policy
Elementary College Chemistry
Fashion Illustration
Fashion Industry
Fitting

Flat Pattern Design
General Psychology
General Textiles
History of Costume
Mass Production Techniques
Personal Fashion Selection
Physics: Light, and Photography
Selection and Care
Tailoring
Textiles
Selection and Care
Weaving

OPTIONS WITHIN MAJOR

General Clothing and Textiles
Fashion Design

Fashion Merchandising

RECOMMENDED HIGH SCHOOL COURSES

Chemistry
Home Economics

Sewing

CAREERS	D.O.T. NUMBER	OUTLOOK	AVERAGE INITIAL SALARY
Bachelor Degrees			
Buyer	162.157-018	Good	$20,000
Clothes Designer	142.061-018	Fair/Good	18,000
Extension Service Specialist	096.127-014	Fair/Good	18,000
Fashion Coordinator	185.157-010	Excellent	22,000
Fashion Designer	141.061-014	Fair	19,000
Fashion Illustrator	141.061-014	Fair	18,000
Fashion Promoter		Fair	20,000
Sales Representative	261.257-030	Good	19,000
Textile Converter	185.167-050	Fair	18,000
Theatre Costume Designer	142.061-050	Fair/Good	19,000
Graduate Degrees			
Professor	090.227-010	Good	25,000

COMMERCIAL ART
DESIGN
PHOTOGRAPHY

Commercial art or design is often a selective program requiring a port-folio which demonstrates past performance. The curriculum itself is performance based requiring considerable studio time. The student must expect to show creative work in several areas. In-depth projects in the student's selected specialties are required later in the training. This program is designed to enhance creativity, craftsmanship, and presentation skills on a professional level.

COURSE REQUIREMENTS

Advertising Design
Color Theory
Corporate Identity Design
Environmental Design
Glass Design
Illustration
Industrial Design
Lighting Techniques
Materials & Components
Metal & Jewelry

Packaging & Poster Design
Presentation Models
Problems in Color
Production Drawing
Publication Design
Rendering Techniques
Space Planning
Theory of Environmental Design
Type as Image

OPTIONS WITHIN MAJOR

Crafts Design
Graphic Design
Illustration

Industrial Design
Interior Design
Photography

RECOMMENDED HIGH SCHOOL COURSES

Art
Biology
English
Graphics
Health

Home Economics
Industrial Arts
Math
Social Sciences

CAREERS	D.O.T. NUMBER	OUTLOOK	AVERAGE INITIAL SALARY
Associate Degrees			
Graphic Artist	979.382-018	Fair/Good	$14,000
Layout Assistant	619.130-030	Fair	16,000
Photograph Retoucher	970.281-018	Fair	13,000
Photographer	143.457-010	Fair	21,000
Bachelor Degrees			
Cloth Designer	142.061-014	Fair	18,000
Commercial Designer	141.081-014	Good	19,000
Fashion Artist	141.061-014	Fair	16,000
Graphic Designer	141.061-018	Good	19,000
Illustrator	141.061-022	Good	19,000
Industrial Designer	142.061-026	Good	21,000
Interior Designer	142.051-014	Fair	18,000
Set Illustrator	141.061-030	Fair	17,000
Teacher	091.227-010	Fair	18,000
Technical Illustrator	141.061-026	Good	22,000
Graduate Degree			
Professor	090.227-010	Fair	25,000

COMMUNICATIONS

Communications deals with the effective transmittal of ideas, feelings and media news. Combining an understanding of the effects of mass media, the behavioral sciences, and communications skills allows the graduate to enter advertising, broadcasting, film making, journalism, government, public relations, speech education and any career dealing with personal and public communications. Although competition is high for many openings, there is constantly a need for creative, accurate and effective means of communication.

COURSE REQUIREMENTS

Advertising
Anthropology
Effects of Mass Media
Film
Human Communications
Interpersonal Communications
Journalism
Linguistics
Mass Communications

Methods of Inquiry
Organizational Communications
Photography
Professional Communication
Experience
Psychology
Public Relations
Sociology
Speech

OPTIONS WITHIN MAJOR

Advertising
Broadcasting
Film Production
Journalism
Journalism Education

Organizational Communication
Photography
Public Relations
Speech

RECOMMENDED HIGH SCHOOL COURSES

English (4 years)
Journalism

Social Sciences
Speech

CAREERS	D.O.T. NUMBER	OUTLOOK	AVERAGE INITIAL SALARY
Associate Degrees			
Layout Assistant	619.130-030	Good	$16,000
Motion Picture Photographer	143.062-022	Fair	25,000
Photographer	143.457-010	Fair/Good	21,000
Photography Director/TV	143.062-010	Good	29,000
Bachelor Degrees			
Advertising Manager	163.167-010	Good	23,000
Copywriter	131.067-014	Fair/Good	16,000
Editor	132.067-014	Good	23,000
Journalist	131.267-018	Fair/Good	20,000
Motion Picture/TV Director	159.167-010	Fair	29,000
Newswriter		Good	21,000
Photo Journalist	143.062-034	Good	19,000
Public Relations Specialist	165.067-010	Good	20,000
Radio/TV Announcer	159.147-010	Fair	18,000
Teacher	091.227-010	Fair/Good	18,000
Graduate Degree			
Professor	090.227-010	Good	26,000

COMMUNITY HEALTH
EDUCATION

The goal of the health educator is to enhance the physical, mental, and social well-being of the public through planning and implementation of programs which increase public awareness and understanding of health problems and their solutions. The public health educator stimulates local leaders toward appropriate health action; assists schools, hospitals, organizations, and firms in planning health education programs; distributes pamphlets, posters, exhibits, and forms; educates by radio, T.V., and press; helps with the evaluation of community health needs; and directs people who need special community services. Employment opportunities are available in private and government health agencies.

COURSE REQUIREMENTS

Advanced First Aid
Community Health
Community Health Education
Consumer Health
Cultural Geography
Drug Use/Abuse
Elementary Human Physiology
Epidemiology
Essentials of Nutrition
Fieldwork in Community Health
First Aid and Safety
Health Education Workshop
Health of the Body System
Health Problems Workshop

Health/Self-Destructive Behavior
Human Physiology
Instructional Media Production
Instructorship in First Aid
Interpersonal Group Process
Medical Sociology
Methods in Health Education
News Writing
North American Indian Today
Organizational Behavior
Public Relations
Safety Education
Social Analysis
Social Statistics

OPTIONS WITHIN MAJOR

Community Health Education

Public Health Education

RECOMMENDED HIGH SCHOOL COURSES

Art   Math
Biology   Social Sciences
Health

CAREERS	D.O.T. NUMBER	OUTLOOK	AVERAGE INITIAL SALARY
Associate Degree			
Health Care Center Worker	070.101-046	Fair	$10,000
Bachelor Degrees			
Community Health Planner		Good/Fair	18,000
Community Health Rep.	079.167-010	Good	18,000
Health Organization Worker	079.117-014	Good	13,000
Health Services Adviser	187.117-050	Good/Exc.	18,000
Nutritionist	096.121-014	Good/Exc.	17,000
Graduate Degrees			
Public Health Administrator		Good	24,000
Professor	090.227-010	Good	25,000

COMPUTER SCIENCE

The computer is being used in nearly every walk of life. Few industries can be found which do not use computers either directly or indirectly. A computer professional must be prepared to deal with the design and implementation of computer systems. Training in computer science ranges from basic systems. The current demand for graduates is very high and the job outlook should remain positive through the next decade.

COURSE REQUIREMENTS

Algorithmic Languages &
Compilers
Analytical Geometry & Calculus
Computers and Society
Computer Organization
Computer Organization and
Programming
Computer Programming
Digital Logic Design

Discrete Structures
Elementary Mathematical Statistics
Information Structures
Operating Systems Design
Operating Systems Principles
Physics
Programming Languages
Seminar in Computer
Science Topics

OPTIONS WITHIN MAJOR

Programming
Software Engineering

Systems Analysis

RECOMMENDED HIGH SCHOOL COURSES

Algebra
Calculus

Computer Science
Trigonometry

CAREERS	D.O.T. NUMBER	OUTLOOK	AVERAGE INITIAL SALARY
Bachelor Degrees			
Business Programmer	020.167-018	Excellent	$24,000
Information Systems			
Programmer	020.187-010	Excellent	23,000
Operator	213.362-010	Excellent	19,000
Programmer	007.167-018	Excellent	23,000
Process Control			
Programmer	020.187-014	Excellent	23,000
Technician	003.161-014	Excellent	20,000
Scientific Programmer	020.167-022	Excellent	25,000
Systems Programmer	003.167-062	Excellent	26,000
Graduate Degrees			
Computer Applications			
Engineer	020.062-010	Excellent	32,000
Systems Analyst	012.167-066	Excellent	33,000
Systems Engineer	003.167-062	Excellent	36,000

DANCE
PHYSICAL EDUCATION

Currently dance is the fastest growing performing art in the nation with audiences expanding six-fold and performances increasing seven-fold over the past several years. The quality, vitality, and uniqueness of American dance not only requires traditional skills but demand imagination, creativity, and true artistic ability. The enthusiasm created among the younger audiences has opened new opportunities for dance majors in teaching, training, and performing.

COURSE REQUIREMENTS

Adaptive/Corrective Physical Ed.
Aerobic Dance
Ballet
Ballroom Dance
Dance Composition
Dance Production
Elementary Human
Folk Dance
General Kinesiology

Human Anatomy
Modern Dance
Physiology
Physiology of Activity
Principles of Physical Education
Social Dance
Statistics
Tap Dance

OPTIONS WITHIN MAJOR

Ballet
Dance Specialization

Professional Dance
Dance/Sports Combination

RECOMMENDED HIGH SCHOOL COURSES

Art
Dance

Fine Arts
Sciences

CAREERS	D.O.T. NUMBER	OUTLOOK	AVERAGE INITIAL SALARY
Bachelor Degrees			
Choreographer	151.027-010	Poor	$25,000
Dance Performer	151.047-010	Fair	11,000
Dance Teacher	151.027-014	Good	18,000
Graduate Degrees			
Professor	090.227-010	Fair	25,000

DENTISTRY

Because of the shortage of dentists in many areas of the country, dentistry is an excellent health care profession to pursue. Following three or four years of undergraduate work (in a variety of possible majors) the students must complete at least four years of professional schooling. Specialization can be considered after graduation.

COURSE REQUIREMENTS

Most students are accepted into dental school with a bachelor degree including the following courses:

Anatomy
Biochemistry
Calculus
Chemistry
English
Genetics

Microbiology
Organic Chemistry
Physics
Physiology
Psychology
Vertebrate Anatomy

Professional schools are a continuation of the above in more depth and with clinical experiences.

RECOMMENDED HIGH SCHOOL COURSES

Algebra
Biology
English (4 years)

Geometry
Physics
Physiology

CAREERS	D.O.T. NUMBER	OUTLOOK	AVERAGE INITIAL SALARY
Graduate Degrees			
Dentist	070.101-010	Excellent	$ 65,000
Oral Pathologist	072.061-010	Excellent	105,000
Oral Surgeon	072.101-018	Excellent	102,000
Orthodontist	072.101-022	Excellent	100,000
Pedontist	072.101-030	Excellent	100,000
Prosthodontist	072.101-034	Excellent	105,000

DESIGN AND ILLUSTRATION

Professionals in these careers play an increasingly important social function in creating corporate, government, and advertising communications. This major is concerned with the organization and combination of format and language. The student spends much time in performance classes and must expect to show creative work in several areas.

COURSE REQUIREMENTS

Advertising Design
Color Theory
Conceptual Drawing
Corporate Identity Design
Design
Environmental Design
Exhibit Design
Graphic Design
Illustration
Industrial Design

Lettering and Calligraphy
Packaging Design
Perceptual Drawing
Publication Design
Reproduction
Three-dimensional Design
Two-dimensional Design
Typography
Visual Communication

OPTIONS WITHIN MAJOR

Exhibit Design
Graphic Design

Illustration

RECOMMENDED HIGH SCHOOL COURSES

Art
English

Graphics
Journalism

CAREERS	D.O.T. NUMBER	OUTLOOK	AVERAGE INITIAL SALARY
Associate Degree			
Graphic Artist	979.382-018	Good	$14,000
Bachelor Degrees			
Advertising Designer	247.387-010	Good	16,000
Commercial Artist	141.061-022	Fair	15,000
Commercial Designer	141.081-014	Good	19,000
Copy Artist	131.167-014	Fair	16,000
Fashion Artist	141.061-014	Good	16,000
Graphic Artist	979.382-018	Good	18,000
Illustrator	141.061-022	Good	19,000
Layout Designer	141.061-018	Good	18,000
Graduate Degree			
Professor	090.227-010	Good	25,000

DESIGN ENGINEERING TECHNOLOGY

Application of graphics technology to engineering design was an outgrowth of the space industry and has been spurred on by industrial needs and demands. Present graduates are qualified to work in various fields of engineering design including consideration of new materials, technical graphics, computer-aided design, architectural design, automated graphics, aeronautical machine design, and special design courses in the strength of materials. Lucrative positions continue to be offered as the national demand for graduates continues to increase.

COURSE REQUIREMENTS

Applied Dynamics and Kinematics
Applied Mechanics
Applied Physics
Basic Computer-assisted
Part Programming
Basic Fluid Power
Computer-Aided Drafting
Descriptive Geometry
Design for Technology
Economy, Society, & Public Policy
Electrical Machines & Controls
Elements of Machines

Engineering Graphics
Manufacturing Processes
Materials Science—Nonmetals
Mechanical Drafting
Physical Metallurgy
Production Operations
Professional Graphic
Application
Scientific Computing
Technical Mathematics
Technical Writing

OPTIONS WITHIN MAJOR

Architectural Design
Automated Graphics
Building Construction
Building Design
Computer-aided Design

Computer Programming
Management in Design
Manufacturing Design
Production Design

RECOMMENDED HIGH SCHOOL COURSES

Chemistry   Math (3 years)
Drafting   Physics
Industrial Shop

CAREERS	D.O.T. NUMBER	OUTLOOK	AVERAGE INITIAL SALARY
Bachelor Degrees			
Architectural Drafter	001.261-010	Good	$17,000
Computer-aided Designer		Excellent	28,000
Computer-aided Drafter		Excellent	26,000
Design Engineer	014.081-010	Good/Exc.	26,000
Engineering Assistant	007.161-018	Good/Exc.	17,000
Industrial Designer	142.061-026	Excellent	22,000
Industrial Engineer Technician	012.267-010	Good	18,000
Systems Programmer	007.167-018	Excellent	26,000
Graduate Degree			
Professor	090.227-010	Good	28,000

DIETETICS

Dietitians plan nutritious and appetizing meals to help people maintain or recover good health. They also supervise the food service personnel who prepare and serve the meals, manage dietetic purchasing and accounting, and give advice on good eating habits. Opportunities for employment are found in hospitals, nursing homes, clinics, colleges and universities, health related agencies, restaurants, Armed Forces, and large companies that provide food service for their employees.

COURSE REQUIREMENTS

Bacteriology
Biochemistry
Chemistry
Clinical Nutrition
Community Nutrition
Data Processing
Dietetics
Economics
Food Chemistry
Food Analysis

Food and Nutrition
Human Anatomy
Human Physiology
Institution Management
Mathematics
Medical Dietetics
Microbiology
Psychology
Sociology

OPTIONS WITHIN MAJOR

Foods and Nutrition
Institution Management

Research dietitian

RECOMMENDED HIGH SCHOOL COURSES

Biology
Business Courses
Chemistry
Health

Home Economics
Mathematics
Physiology
Psychology

CAREERS	D.O.T. NUMBER	OUTLOOK	AVERAGE INITIAL SALARY
Bachelor Degrees			
Clinical Dietitian	077.127-014	Good/Exc.	$19,000
Dietetic Educators	077.127-022	Good/Exc.	18,000
Nutritionist	077.127-010	Good/Exc.	18,000
Graduate Degrees			
Administrative Dietitian	077.117-010	Good/Exc.	25,000
Professor	090.227-010	Good/Exc.	27,000
Public Health Nutritionist	077.127-010	Good/Exc.	21,000
Research Dietitian	077.061-010	Good/Exc.	25,000

DRAFTING

Drafting technicians assist engineers, architects, and designers with sketches, calculations, specifications, and materials needed on the job. Employment opportunities in industry, architects' offices, or government agencies involves use and knowledge of handbooks, tables, calculators automated drafting machines, and traditional drafting equipment. The demand for drafters will increase as supporting personnel to engineers and scientists and in performing liaison work between the professional and nonprofessional people.

COURSE REQUIREMENTS

Commercial Structures
Computer-aided Design
Computer-assisted Drafting
Descriptive Geometry
Elements of Machines
Engineering Graphics
Graphics

Mechanical Drafting
Perspective
Professional Graphics Application
Residential Drafting
Residential Drafting
Technical Math

OPTIONS WITHIN MAJOR

Architectural Drafting
Computer-aided Technology

Mechanical Drafting

RECOMMENDED HIGH SCHOOL COURSES

Drafting
Math (3 years)

Physics

CAREERS	D.O.T. NUMBER	OUTLOOK	AVERAGE INITIAL SALARY
Associate Degrees			
Castings Drafter	007.261-014	Fair	$16,000
Directional Drafter	010.281-010	Good	16,000
Drafter	007.161-018	Good	17,000
Electrical Drafter	003.281-010	Good	17,000
Electronics Drafter	003.281-014	Good	17,000
Engineering Technician	003.367-018	Good	17,000
Patent Drafter	007.261-018	Good	19,000
Tool Design Drafter	007.261-022	Good	16,000
Bachelor Degrees			
Aeronautical Drafter	002.261-010	Good	23,000
Automobile Design Drafter	017.281-022	Good	21,000
Cartographic Drafter	018.261-022	Good	18,000
Civil Drafter	005.281-014	Good	20,000
Design Drafter	017.261-014	Good/Exc.	23,000
Geological Drafter	010.281-014	Fair/Good	16,000
Geophysical Drafter	010.281-018	Fair/Good	16,000
Mechanical Drafter	007.281-022	Excellent	18,000
Structural Drafter	005.281-014	Excellent	19,000
Topographical Drafter	018.261-014	Good	18,000

EARLY CHILDHOOD EDUCATION

Early childhood education combines a knowledge of basic developmental and behavioral characteristics of the child with appropriate teaching skills to prepare students to become preschool and elementary teachers, or effective parents. As the early stages of education set the future pattern for many students, well-qualified instructors are in demand despite the abundance of elementary teachers in many areas of the country. Although many students teach in the public or private schools, a great number of graduates find training in early childhood education an asset in their home, community, and church life.

COURSE REQUIREMENTS

Art
Child Development
Child Psychology
Children's Literature
Geography
Math
Music for Elementary Teachers

Physical Education
Skill Analysis and Rhythm/Dance
School Health
Student Teaching
The Child in the Family
World Affairs

OPTIONS WITHIN MAJOR

Early Childhood Education
Elementary School

Kindergarten
Preschool

RECOMMENDED HIGH SCHOOL COURSES

Home Economics
Psychology

Sociology

CAREERS	D.O.T. NUMBER	OUTLOOK	AVERAGE INITIAL SALARY
Bachelor Degrees			
Day Care Center Worker	359.677-018	Fair/Good	$13,000
Elementary Teacher	092.227-018	Good	18,000
Kindergarten Teacher	092.227-014	Good	18,000
Nursery School Director	092.137-010	Fair	16,000
Pre-school Teacher	092.227-014	Good	18,000
Graduate Degrees (M.S.)			
Counselor	095.107-014	Good	23,000
Professor	090.227-010	Fair	28,000

ECONOMICS

The study of economics provides a broad view of national and international business conditions and an understanding of production, distribution and consumption. It provides businessmen and government officials with vital information on matters such as prices, markets, domestic and foreign trade and government policies. Students majoring in economics have considerable latitude in occupation selection. Graduates often pursue law school, graduate work in business (MBA), or economics as well as going into business or government service.

COURSE REQUIREMENTS

Calculus
Econometrics
Economic Analysis of Decision
Economic, Society and Public Policy
Theory of Price

Mathematical Statistics
Quantitative Methods
Statistics
Theory of Income
Math

OPTIONS WITHIN MAJOR

Applied Economics

Economic Theory

RECOMMENDED HIGH SCHOOL COURSES

Algebra
English

Trigonometry

CAREERS	D.O.T. NUMBER	OUTLOOK	AVERAGE INITIAL SALARY
Bachelor Degrees			
Market Research Analyst	050.067-014	Good/Exc.	$24,000
Stock Broker	251.157-010	Good	31,000
Graduate Degrees			
Business Market Research Analyst	050.067-014	Good/Exc.	29,000
Economist	050.067-010	Good/Exc.	31,000
Government Economist	050.067-010	Good/Exc.	29,000
Professor	090.227-010	Good/Exc.	29,000

EDUCATIONAL PSYCHOLOGY

Educational psychology offers programs which prepare students to teach in special education settings dealing with intellectual handicaps, behavior disorders, speech or auditory disabilities, and other communicative or learning problems. Certification is required for those desiring to teach in the public schools and can be incorporated with a regular four-year program. Owing to national legislation, which requires free, appropriate education for all handicapped children, the demand for special education teachers, administrators, and personnel to provide training has increased significantly. To meet the needs of the handicapped and to fulfill these requirements, qualified graduates should be in demand for some time to come.

COURSE REQUIREMENTS

Audiology
Behavior Modifications
Behavior Problems
Communicative Disorders
Development & Learning
Exceptional Children
Group Counseling

Mental Retardation
Phonetics
School Guidance
School Psychology
Sign Language
Testing Techniques

OPTIONS WITHIN MAJOR

Counseling
Intellectually Handicapped
Learning Disabilities

School Psychology
Teaching Emotionally

RECOMMENDED HIGH SCHOOL COURSES

English
Math
Psychology

Sociology
Speech

CAREERS	D.O.T. NUMBER	OUTLOOK	AVERAGE INITIAL SALARY
Bachelor Degrees			
Learning Specialist	094.227-022	Excellent	$18,000
Resource Teacher	094.227-018	Excellent	18,000
Special Education Teacher	094.227-018	Excellent	18,000
Teacher — of the Mentally Retarded	094.227-022	Excellent	18,000
Therapist for the Blind	076.221-010	Fair	15,000
Graduate Degrees			
Career Assessment Officer		Good	21,000
Career Counselor	045.167-042	Good/Exc.	24,000
Counseling Psychologist	045.107-026	Good	26,000
Counselor	045.107-010	Good/Exc.	23,000
Director of Counseling	045.107-018	Fair/Good	30,000
Director of Guidance	045.117-010	Fair/Good	30,000
Educational Psychologist	045.107-010	Good	26,000
Mental Health Counselor		Fair	24,000
Professor	090.227-010	Good	27,000
School Counselor	045.107-010	Good	23,000
School Psychologist	045.067-010	Good	25,000
State Rehabilitation Counselor	045.167-042	Fair	20,000
Substance Abuse Counselor		Good/Exc.	21,000

ELECTRICAL ENGINEERING

Electrical engineers apply a thorough knowledge of electricity and education in physics, chemistry, and mathematics to develop systems and equipment used in the generation, transmittal, and reception of information and energy. Solid state electronic devices must be designed for thousands of new applications each year. Current demands on resources for more electrical power, communications systems, and computer systems increase the need for electrical engineers. The need for thousands more in the field of electrical engineering and technical manpower requirements provide many opportunities for men and women alike.

COURSE REQUIREMENTS

Analytical Geometry/Calculus
Applied Ordinary Differential
Equations
Circuit Analysis
College Chemistry
Computer Engineering
Digital Computer Electronics
Electric Circuit Numerical Solutions
Electrical Circuits/Devices
Electrical Energy Conversion

Electrical Engineering
Elements of Thermoscience
Engineering Graphics
Engineering Mechanics-
Dynamics
Engineering Mechanics-Statis
Feedback Concepts
Numerical Solutions in Electrical
Engineering
Principles of Physics

OPTIONS WITHIN MAJOR

Electrical Power
Computer
Electronics

Power
Solid-state Communications

RECOMMENDED HIGH SCHOOL COURSES

Algebra
Chemistry
Physics

Plane Geometry
Trigonometry

CAREERS	D.O.T. NUMBER	OUTLOOK	AVERAGE INITIAL SALARY
Bachelor Degrees			
Applications Engineer	020.062-010	Good	$24,000
Communications Engr.	828.261-010	Good	23,000
Design Engineer	003.061-018	Good	26,000
Electrical Engineer	003.061-010	Excellent	30,000
Electrical Test Engineer	003.061-014	Good	28,000
Electro-optical Engineer	023.061-010	Good	22,000
Electronics Engineer	003.061-030	Excellent	32,000
Electronics Test Engr.	003.061-042	Good	29,000
Power/Solid State Engr.	003.167-018	Excellent	29,000
Graduate Degrees			
Administration/Management Engineer		Good/Exc.	35,000
Consulting Engineer		Good	37,000
Development & Research Engineer	003.061-026	Excellent	37,000
Engineering Professor	090.227-010	Excellent	31,000
Systems Engineer	003.167-062	Excellent	36,000

ELECTRONICS ENGINEERING TECHNOLOGY

Electronics engineering technologists apply electronic devices and systems to the control of equipment in industry, laboratories, and the home. Graduates are prepared to enter shipbuilding, medical electronics, research laboratories, aerospace industries, communication, computer productions, and a variety of industries on the basis of their knowledge of electronic circuit principles, equipment operations, and digital computer hardware and software. Electronic technicians (with 2-year degrees) are prepared to assist engineers with practical and detailed work in any of the industries listed above. Because of the rapid increase in digital computer use in all walks of life, as well as other essential contributions of electronics, the occupational opportunities in this field are tremendous.

COURSE REQUIREMENTS

Analytical Geometry
Applied Physics
Audio Communications Systems
Calculus
Communications Circuits
Communications Systems
Computer Aided Instrumentation
Computer Science
Control Systems
Data Transmission
DC and AC Circuits
Digital Circuits
Digital Electronics
Economics
Electrical Drawing
Electronic Instrumentation

Electrical Trouble Shooting
Electronic Fabrication & Assembly
Electronical Control Systems
Electronics
High Frequency Systems
Industrial Electronics
Linear Integrated Circuits
Minicomputer Application
Process Control Computers
Physics
Radio Broadcast Systems
Real-time Computer Systems
Technical Math
Technical Writing
T.V. Broadcast Systems

OPTIONS WITHIN MAJOR

Circuit Analysis
Communications
Computer-aided Processes
Digital Electronics

Electronic Technology
Instrumentation
Minicomputer Applications

RECOMMENDED HIGH SCHOOL COURSES

Electrical Shop   Physics
Math (3 years)

CAREERS	D.O.T. NUMBER	OUTLOOK	AVERAGE INITIAL SALARY
Associate Degrees			
Electrical Power Tech.	720.281-018	Good/Exc.	$18,000
Electronics Technician	003.161-014	Excellent	19,000
Bachelor Degrees			
Communications Engineer	828.261-010	Good	22,000
Communications Technologist	003.161-014	Good/Exc.	23,000
Computer Designer		Good/Exc.	24,000
Computer Technologist	726.131-010	Good/Exc.	26,000
Electronics Engineer	003.061-030	Excellent	27,000
Electronics Systems Mgr.	828.161-010	Fair	21,000
Electronic Systems Specialist		Good/Exc.	25,000
Electronics Test Engineer	003.061-014	Good	29,000
Process Control Programmer		Good	22,000
Television & Audio Systems Specialist	726.281-014	Excellent	20,000
Graduate Degree			
Professor	090.227-010	Good	25,000

ELEMENTARY EDUCATION

Elementary school teachers face the awesome challenge of teaching a diversity of subject matter to young minds in an effort to mold and prepare them for life's future challenges. A variety of experiences is to be had throughout the United States, but in some areas the supply of elementary teachers exceeds the demand. Despite the numbers available, there is still a great need for innovative, excellent elementary teachers.

COURSE REQUIREMENTS

Art for Elementary Grades
Basic Concepts of Math
Child Development
Educational Psychology
Elementary Music Methods
Geography

Instructional Methods
P.E.-Primary Grades
School Health
School Law
World Affairs

OPTIONS WITHIN MAJOR

Teaching

RECOMMENDED HIGH SCHOOL COURSES

Art
Biology
English (4 years)
History

Math
Music
Psychology
Science

CAREERS	D.O.T. NUMBER	OUTLOOK	AVERAGE INITIAL SALARY
Bachelor Degrees			
Audiovisual Specialist	100.167-010	Fair	$18,000
Teacher	091.227-010	Good/Exc.	18,000
Graduate Degrees			
Administrator	099.117-026	Fair/Good	38,000
Principal	099.117-018	Fair	38,000

ENGLISH

Although accurate usage of the English language is essential to the college graduate, encountering the humanizing forces of languages and literature is the primary objective of the English major. The graduate of English is prepared for numerous career possibilities including teaching, business, law or graduate school. The combined liberal arts and analytical and writing skill preparation is useful in most graduate studies as well as library science, communications, and journalism. The demand for English teachers still exceeds the supply of graduates each year, and other students are finding success in related fields.

COURSE REQUIREMENTS

American Literature
Creative Writing
Critical & Interpretive Writing
Drama
English
Exposition & Report Writing

Folklore
Grammar
Novel
Science Fiction
Semantics
Short Story

OPTIONS WITHIN MAJOR

Professional Writing

Teaching

RECOMMENDED HIGH SCHOOL COURSES

English
Foreign Language
Humanities

Literature
Writing

CAREERS	D.O.T. NUMBER	OUTLOOK	AVERAGE INITIAL SALARY
Bachelor Degrees			
Book Editor	132.067-014	Fair	$24,000
Copywriter	131.067-014	Fair/Good	16,000
Critic	131.067-018	Fair	30,000
Editor	132.067-014	Fair	23,000
Newspaper Editor	132.017-014	Fair	24,000
Poet	131.067-042	Poor/Fair	Varies
Proofreader		Fair/Good	14,000
Prose Writer	131.067-040	Good	Varies
Publications Editor	132.037-022	Good	23,000
Screen Writer	131.087-018	Good	25,000
Story Editor	132.037-026	Poor	18,000
Teacher	091.227-010	Good	18,000
Technical Scientific Editor	132.017-018	Good	24,000
Technical Writer	131.267-026	Fair/Good	22,000
Graduate Degree			
Professor	090.227-010	Good	25,000

ENVIRONMENTAL HEALTH

Environmental health involves the application of science and education in the prevention of disease and injury. Environmentalists deal with the identification and correction of health problems involving water, soil, and air pollution, and waste and sewage disposal. They manage the quality of milk, food and drugs, the control of rodents, and insects, and various pests. They also work with radiation and noise hazards, effective housing and space utilization, sanitation of schools and institutions, and infection control in hospitals and other public facilities. Employment opportunities should remain positive with local, state, and federal departments of health with hospitals and health care operations, and in industry.

COURSE REQUIREMENTS

Basic Computers
Community Health
Environmental Health
Environmental Physics
Epidemiology
Fieldwork in Public Health
Food Microbiology
General Microbiology
Health of the Body Systems

Human Parasitology
Human Physiology
Leadership Development
Occupational/Industrial Health
Organic Chemistry
Safety Education
State/Local Government Policy
Statistics
Water/Sewage Microbiology

OPTIONS WITHIN MAJOR

Government Agencies

Industrial Staff

RECOMMENDED HIGH SCHOOL COURSES

Biology
Chemistry
Health

Math (3 years)
Physical Science

CAREERS	D.O.T. NUMBER	OUTLOOK	AVERAGE INITIAL SALARY
Bachelor Degrees			
Community Health Planner		Fair/Good	$17,000
Environmental Health Specialist	029.261-014	Fair	17,000
Food & Drug Inspector	168.267-042	Fair	16,000
Food Technologist	041.081-010	Good	25,000
Health Care Inspector	168.167-042	Fair	17,000
Health & Safety Inspector	168.167-062	Fair	17,000
Industrial Hygienist	079.061-010	Fair/Good	28,000
Pollution Control Officer	029.061-014	Good	16,000
Public Health Officer	168.167-018	Good/Exc.	16,000
Public Health Worker	187.117-050	Fair	16,000
Quality Control Officer	168.167-066	Fair	17,000
Sanitation Officer	079.117-018	Fair	18,000
Graduate Degrees			
Environmental Scientist		Good	22,000
Professor	090.227-010	Fair	26,000

EUROPEAN STUDIES

European Studies is an interdisciplinary program typically referred to as "Area Studies." It integrates ideas and principles from anthropology, literature, history, geography, and economics. This broadly based education allows one to do historical research, social, political, and economic analysis, and literary criticism. Students often continue on to advanced studies in law, business administration and liberal arts, or may become involved in teaching or government service.

COURSE REQUIREMENTS

Arts in the Western Culture
Baroque Art
Comparative Economic Systems
Comparative Literature
Contemporary European Art
Cultural Geography
Economic Analysis
Economic History of Europe
English Literature
European Art and Architecture
European Geography
French Literature
Geography and World Affairs
German Literature

History of Musical Style
Italian Art
Italian Literature
International Trade and Finance
Nineteenth Century Europe
Origins of Western Philosophy
Political Geography
Renaissance Art
Romantic Music
The Age of Enlightenment
The Reformation
The Renaissance
Twentieth Century Europe
World Civilizations

OPTIONS WITHIN MAJOR

Business
Culture
Geography

Government
Philosophy

RECOMMENDED HIGH SCHOOL COURSES

Art
Economics
English
Foreign Language

Geography
History
Literature

CAREERS	D.O.T. NUMBER	OUTLOOK	AVERAGE INITIAL SALARY
Bachelor Degrees			
Biographer	052.067-010	Fair/Poor	Varies
Correspondent	131.267-018	Fair	$23,000
Foreign Service Officer	188.117-106	Fair	22,000
Historian	052.067-022	Fair/Poor	21,000
Import/Export Agent	184.117-022	Good	22,000
Intelligence Expert	059.267-010	Good	24,000
Public Relations Specialist	165.067-010	Fair	25,000
Publications Editor	132.037-026	Poor	16,000
Travel Agent	225.157-010	Good	14,000
Graduate Degrees			
Foreign Service	051.067-010	Good	27,000
Professor	090.227-010	Good	27,000
Researcher	052.167-010	Good	25,000

FAMILY RESOURCE MANAGEMENT

Family resource management consists of training in the development of managerial skills directly related to financial security, consumer satisfaction, and successful family living. The practical skills and knowledge obtained serves the individual and opens employment opportunities in finance, education, social services, government, business, and any other area that requires consumer and family finance, home management, or household equipment specialization. Increasing possibilities are available with government agencies, educational institutions, financial firms, and private companies of all sorts. Various opportunities are also opening up in foreign nations to train and assist populations in basic management skills.

COURSE REQUIREMENTS

Consumer Behavior
Consumer Law
Economics of Consumption
Family & Consumer Economics
Family Estate Planning
Family Financial Analysis

Family Management
Family Money Management
Housing and Lighting
Housing Equipment
Residence Management
Space Planning

OPTIONS WITHIN MAJOR

Consumer Affairs
Equipment, Foods, Housing

Family Financial Planning
Family Management

RECOMMENDED HIGH SCHOOL COURSES

Economics
Family Living
Personal Finance

Psychology
Sociology

CAREERS	D.O.T. NUMBER	OUTLOOK	AVERAGE INITIAL SALARY
Bachelor Degrees			
Consumer Affairs Staff	096.121-014	Fair	$18,000
Estate Planner	186.167-010	Excellent	28,000
Extension Service Specialist	096.127-014	Fair	25,000
Family Financial Planning & Counseling	169.267-018	Good	19,000
Family/Social Services Staff		Fair	16,000
Kitchen Designer Demonstrator		Fair	13,000
Graduate Degree			
Professor	090.227-010	Good	27,000

FINANCE AND BANKING

Commercial banks constitute one of the fastest growing industries in our economy. Because banks employ specialized techniques and equipment in very detailed work, most employees gain experience and skill through on-the-job training. Banks usually seek college graduates for officer trainee jobs. However, many openings exists for high school graduates in other bank positions. Bank employees generally have good opportunities for advancement.

COURSE REQUIREMENTS

Administrative Data Processing
Business in Urban Society
Business Statistics
Capital Budgeting
Finance Management
Industrial Operations Management
Introduction to Accounting

Investment Finance
Managerial Accounting
Managerial Economics
Money and Banking
Principles of Finance
Principles of Marketing
Investment Finance

OPTIONS WITHIN MAJOR

Banking
Finance

Insurance

RECOMMENDED HIGH SCHOOL COURSES

Accounting
Bookkeeping
Business Machine Operation

Commercial Law
Computer Operation
Data Processing

CAREERS	D.O.T. NUMBER	OUTLOOK	AVERAGE INITIAL SALARY
Bachelor Degrees			
Assistant Vice-president	186.117-078	Good	$31,000
Broker	250.357-018	Good/Exc.	28,000
Chief Executive Officers & President	186.117-054	Good	38,000
Controller	186.117-014	Fair	25,000
Estate Planner	186.167-010	Excellent	28,000
Financial Aids Officer	090.117-030	Fair	24,000
Financial Analyst	020.167-014	Good	24,000
Loan Officer	186.267-018	Good	24,000
Senior & Executive Vice-president	186.117-078	Good	35,000
Treasurer	161.117-018	Fair	23,000
Trust Officer	186.117-074	Good	25,000
Underwriter	169.167-058	Good	22,000

FOOD SCIENCE

Food science deals with the application of biological, physical, and social sciences in solving world food and nutritional problems. A study of food production from raw food sources allows a student to prepare for professional vocations such as directing food quality, researching and developing new foods, managing food processing inspection, working in test kitchens, or serving as a medical dietitian. Nutritionists work in health-related services in the community, state, or nation and as consultants for private pharmaceutical or food industries. The food scientist deals more with the research, quality control, and inspection of products in the food industry.

COURSE REQUIREMENTS

Biochemistry
Chemistry
Clinical Nutrition
College Algebra
Community Nutrition
Dietetics
Experimental Human Nutrition
Experiments in Nutrition
Family Money Management
Food Analysis
Food Chemistry
Food Microbiology
Food Preservation

Food Production
Food Processing
Food Quality Preservation
Food Research/Development
Food Science
Human Anatomy
Human Nutrition
Human Physiology
Medical Dietetics
Microbiology
Organization Behavior
Physics
Quantitative/Qualitative Analysis

OPTIONS WITHIN MAJOR

Food Science
Food Systems Administration

Medical Dietetics
Nutrition

RECOMMENDED HIGH SCHOOL COURSES

Biology
Botany
Business
Chemistry

English
Math
Physics

CAREERS	D.O.T. NUMBER	OUTLOOK	AVERAGE INITIAL SALARY
Bachelor Degrees			
Dietitian	077.117-010	Fair/Good	$19,000
Food Chemist	022.061-014	Fair	23,000
Food Systems Mgt.	187.167-026	Good	20,000
Food Technologist	041.081-010	Good	25,000
Public Health Officer	187.117-050	Good	16,000
Quality Control Officer	168.167-066	Fair	17,000
Teacher	091.227-010	Fair	18,000
Test Kitchen Specialist		Fair	13,000
Graduate Degrees			
Food Scientist	041.081-010	Good	24,000
Professor	090.227-010	Good	26,000

FORESTRY

Foresters plan and supervise the growing, protection, and utilization of trees. They make maps of forest areas, estimate the amount of standing timber and future growth, and manage timber sales. Other duties may range from wildlife protection and watershed management to supervision of camps, parks, and grazing lands. They must deal constantly with land owners, loggers, forestry aids, and a wide variety of other people. Qualified foresters find job opportunities available with private industry, the Forest Service of the Department of Agriculture, state and local governments, college and universities, and consulting firms.

COURSE REQUIREMENTS

Arboriculture
Dendrology
Field Studies
Forest Ecology
Forest Economics
Forest Management
Forest Protection

Forest Soils
Forestry
Harvesting Systems
Quantitative Methods
Tree Pathology
Wood Properties

OPTIONS WITHIN MAJOR

Forestry
Recreation

Tree Nursery

RECOMMENDED HIGH SCHOOL COURSES

Chemistry
English Literature

Physics
Public Speaking

CAREERS	D.O.T. NUMBER	OUTLOOK	AVERAGE INITIAL SALARY
Associate Degree			
Forestry Technician	040.061-062	Fair/Good	$14,000
Bachelor Degrees			
Forest Ecologist	040.061-030	Fair	17,000
Forest Ranger	040.061-034	Fair/Good	17,000
Graduate Degrees			
M.S. Degree Forester		Good/Exc.	23,000
PhD. Forester		Good/Exc.	29,000
Professor/Research	090.227-010	Fair	26,000

FRENCH

Students majoring in French prepare in language, culture, and literature for international business, banking, trade, airlines or related professions in French-speaking nations (France, Switzerland, Belgium, and Canada). Teaching positions are also available in some areas, and many graduate and professional studies (medicine, etc.) require students to learn a foreign language. Many firms, as well as government agencies, are looking for someone who can communicate and think independently in more than one language.

COURSE REQUIREMENTS

Composition
Conversation
Cultural Civilization
French

Grammar
Literature
Phonetics
Translation

OPTIONS WITHIN MAJOR

Business
Education

Translation Interpretation

RECOMMENDED HIGH SCHOOL COURSES

French
Geography
History

Humanities
Literature
Social Science

CAREERS	D.O.T. NUMBER	OUTLOOK	AVERAGE INITIAL SALARY
Bachelor Degrees			
Customs Official	168.267-022	Fair	$16,000
Foreign Service Officer	188.117-106	Fair	22,000
Import/Export Agent	184.117-022	Good	22,000
Intelligence Expert	059.267-010	Good	24,000
Interpreter	137.267-010	Good	19,000
Language Researcher	059.067-014	Fair	22,000
Public Relations Specialist	165.067-010	Fair	25,000
Scientific Writer		Fair	24,000
Teacher	019.227-010	Good	18,000
Translator	137.267-018	Good	19,000
Travel Agent	225.157-010	Good	12,000
Graduate Degrees			
Professor	090.227-010	Good	25,000
Scientific Linguist	059.067-014	Fair	24,000

GENEALOGY

An upsurge across the nation has increased genealogical interest and research, both on a private and on a professional basis. Genealogy deals with searching, locating, recording, and preserving records of persons and families living or deceased. Currently, training is offered in two-year programs for individual needs to train professionals. Although career opportunities are limited, a degree in genealogy can prepare students for advanced studies in related fields.

COURSE REQUIREMENTS

Genealogy	History
Geographical History	Paleography
Geography	Research Methods

OPTIONS WITHIN MAJOR

Family Research	Professional Genealogy
Individual Research	

RECOMMENDED HIGH SCHOOL COURSES

English	Social Studies
Foreign Language	

CAREERS	D.O.T. NUMBER	OUTLOOK	AVERAGE INITIAL SALARY
Associate Degrees			
Genealogy Research Specialist	052.067-018	Fair/Poor	$16,000
Librarian	100.127-014	Fair	19,000

GEOGRAPHY

Geography is the science of spatial analysis concerned primarily with interpreting the occurrence, distribution, and interrelationships of the physical and cultural patterns which can be discerned. Employment is available in many areas of private business and industry, government agencies, and education as cartographers, geographic analysts, land officers, climatologists, intelligence specialists, economists, and teachers. Excellent employment opportunities exist in city and region planning, industrial location research, and teaching on several levels.

COURSE REQUIREMENTS

Air Photo Interpretation
Biogeograhpy
Climatology
Earth Ecosystems
Economic Geography
Geographics
geographic Field Techniques
Geography

Geography of Culture
Geomorphology
Hydrology
Land Use Planning
Maps & Air Photos
Resource Management
Soils
World Vegetation

OPTIONS WITHIN MAJOR

Cartography
Geographic Planning

Teaching
Travel/Tourism

RECOMMENDED HIGH SCHOOL COURSES

Foreign Language
Geography

Natural Science
Social Studies

CAREERS	D.O.T. NUMBER	OUTLOOK	AVERAGE INITIAL SALARY
Associate Degrees			
Planning/Cartographic Technician	018.261-026	Good	$17,000
Travel Agent	252.157-010	Good	12,000
Bachelor Degrees			
Cartographer	018.261-010	Good	20,000
Climatologist		Fair/Good	17,000
Industrial Location Geographer		Excellent	21,000
Map Curator		Fair/Good	22,000
Marketing Research Specialist	050.067-014	Good/Exc.	24,000
Teacher	091.227-010	Good	18,000
Travel/Tourism	252.157-010	Excellent	19,000
Urban, Region Planner	199.167-014	Good	22,000
Graduate Degrees			
Geographer	029.067-010	Good	27,000
Environmental Researcher	029.167-014	Good	24,000
Physical Geographer	029.067-014	Good	27,000
Professor	090.227-010	Good	27,000

GEOLOGY

Geology involves the study of a wide variety of topics dealing with earth and life sciences. Geologists use a spectrum of knowledge from physics, chemistry, mathematics, botany, zoology, and related fields. They deal with energy, mineral research and discovery, environmental geology, oceanography, and other outdoor field studies or indoor laboratory investigations. Engineering geologists apply geological principles to a variety of projects including highways, dams, reservoirs, tunnels, pipelines, subdivisions, power plants, land-use planning, and related areas. Students of geology who tend toward earth science can prepare for a composite science teaching career on the secondary level. Job opportunities are available in industry, in academic areas, and in government agencies throughout the world.

COURSE REQUIREMENTS

Algebra
Analytical Geometry
Astrogeology
Calculus
Chemistry
Earth Processes
Economic Geology
Geological Literature
Geological Methods
Geomorphology
Historical Geology
Inorganic Chemistry

Marine Geology
Mineralogy
Optical Mineralogy
Organic Chemistry
Paleontology
Petrology
Physical Geology
Principles of Physics
Sedimentation
Stratigraphy
Structural Geology
Trigonometry

OPTIONS WITHIN MAJOR

Earth Science
Engineer Geology

Geology

RECOMMENDED HIGH SCHOOL COURSES

Chemistry
Computer Science

Math (3 years)
Physics

99

CAREERS	D.O.T. NUMBER	OUTLOOK	AVERAGE INITIAL SALARY
Bachelor Degrees			
Geodesist	024.061-014	Fair/Good	$21,000
Geologist		Excellent	21,000
Groundwater Engineer		Good	24,000
Hydrologist	024.061-034	Fair	19,000
Land Use Planner	199.167-014	Good	22,000
Mineralologist	024.061-038	Good/Exc.	21,000
Mining Geologist/Engineer	024.061-019	Excellent	28,000
Seismologist	024.061-050	Good	23,000
Stratigrapher	024.061-051	Fair/Good	20,000
Teacher	091.227-010	Good	18,000
Graduate Degrees			
Geophysicist	024.061-030	Good	25,000
Paleontologist	024.061-042	Good	26,000
Petroleum Geologist	024.061-022	Excellent	28,000
Petroleum Geologist Engineer	024.061-018	Excellent	33,000
Petrologist	024.061-046	Fair/Good	25,000
Professor	090.227-010	Fair	28,000
Research	024.061-023	Good	29,000

GEOPHYSICS

Geophysicists study the composition and physical aspects of the earth and its electric, magnetic, and gravitational fields. They often use satellites to conduct tests from outer space and computers to collect and analyze data. Geophysicists usually specialize in one of three general phases of the science—solid earth, fluid earth, or upper atmosphere. Some may also study other planets.

Most geophysicists work in private industry, chiefly for petroleum or natural gas companies. Others are in mining companies, exploration and consulting firms, and research institutes. A few are independent consultants and some do geophysical prospecting on a fee or contract basis. Many geophysicists, and hydrologists work for Federal Government agencies, mainly the U. S. Geological Survey, the National Oceanic and Atmospheric Administration, and the Defense Department. Other geophysicists work for colleges and universities, state governments, and nonprofit research institutions.

COURSE REQUIREMENTS

Chemistry	Geophysics
Climates	Gravity Fields
Experimental Geology	Instrumentation
Experimental Petrology	Isotope Geochemistry
Exploration Geophysics	Magnetic Fields
Geographics	Minerals
Geomorphology	Physics
Geophysical Exploration	Seismic Waves

OPTIONS WITHIN MAJOR

Industrial Geophysics	Teaching
Research	

RECOMMENDED HIGH SCHOOL COURSES

Chemistry	Mathematics
Earth Science	Physics
Geology	

101

CAREERS	D.O.T. NUMBER	OUTLOOK	AVERAGE INITIAL SALARY
Bachelor Degrees			
Geodesist	024.061-014	Excellent	$21,000
Hydrologist	024.061-034	Fair	19,000
Seismologist	024.061-050	Good	23,000
Stratigrapher	024.061-054	Good	20,000
Graduate Degrees			
Geophysicist	024.061-030	Excellent	25,000
Paleomagnetician	024.061-042	Excellent	27,000
Paleontologist	024.061-042	Good	26,000
Professor	090.227-010	Good	29,000

GERMAN

A study of German provides the student with a broad liberal arts background for specialized graduate study or teaching at the secondary level. Because of the shortage of teaching positions, many language majors are turning to law, medicine, or international business and law. Many industrial firms and government agencies are seeking graduates who are proficient in a second language and understanding of another culture.

COURSE REQUIREMENTS

Conversation
Composition
Cultural Civilization
German

Grammar
Literature
Phonetics
Translation

OPTIONS WITHIN MAJOR

Business
Education

Interpretation
Translation

RECOMMENDED HIGH SCHOOL COURSES

Geography
German
History

Humanities
Literature
Social Science

CAREERS	D.O.T. NUMBER	OUTLOOK	AVERAGE INITIAL SALARY
Bachelor Degrees			
Customs Official	168.267-022	Fair	$16,000
Foreign Service Officer	188.117-106	Fair	22,000
Import/Export	184.117-022	Good	22,000
Intelligence Expert	059.267-010	Good	24,000
Interpreter	137.267-010	Fair/Good	19,000
Language Researcher	059.067-014	Fair	22,000
Public Relations Specialist	165.067-010	Fair	25,000
Scientific Writer		Fair	24,000
Teacher	019.227-010	Good	18,000
Translator	137.267-018	Good	19,000
Travel Agent	225.157-010	Good	12,000
Graduate Degrees			
Professor	090.227-010	Good	25,000
Scientific Linguist	059.067-014	Fair	24,000

HEALTH ADMINISTRATION

Administrators in health care, work with medical doctors, nurses, and other professionals. In addition, they are responsible for proper care of the patients. The needs of the health institution are another responsibility of the administrator. A variety of facilities offer extended care, short-term care, emergency, same-day service, or a combination of some or all of these. Health care is undergoing dramatic changes. Dynamic and diversified management is needed to provide the leadership required in new and pioneering efforts.

COURSE REQUIREMENTS

Computers for Managers
Cooperative Education
Ethics
Financial Accounting
Financial Management
Health Financial Management
Health Service Economics
Health Service Organizations
Labor Relations
Legal Concepts
Marketing and Planning

Marketing Health Services
Medical Care
Operations Management
Oral Communications
Organizational Development
Personnel Management
Quantitative Analysis
Risk Analysis
Strategic Planning
Written Communication

OPTIONS WITHIN MAJOR

Clinic Administration

Hospital Administration

RECOMMENDED HIGH SCHOOL COURSES

Algebra

English

CAREERS	D.O.T. NUMBER	OUTLOOK	AVERAGE INITIAL SALARY
Graduate Degrees			
Hospital Administrator	187.117-010	Excellent	$34,000
Medical Facilities Director	188.117-082	Excellent	35,000
Professor	090.227-010	Excellent	27,000

HEALTH SCIENCE

Personal and public health are of major importance today, and educating young people about proper health and health problems is challenging and rewarding. Medical costs, drug abuse, venereal disease, quackery, and a multitude of health-related concerns provide a vast amount of information to be taught in the public schools. Accident prevention and treatment, as well as dealing with many of the problems of today's youth, provide challenges and make health education an interesting field.

COURSE REQUIREMENT

Advanced First Aid Instructorship
Consumer Health
Drug Use and Abuse
Elementary Human Anatomy
Elementary Human Physiology
Essentials of Nutrition
Health Education
Health Service Teaching Methods

Human Heredity
Human Nutrition
Human Sexuality
Microbiology
Personal Health
Psychology of Adolescence
Safety Education
School Health/Community

OPTIONS WITHIN MAJOR

Education

Governmental Agencies

RECOMMENDED HIGH SCHOOL COURSES

Biology
Chemistry

Math

CAREERS	D.O.T. NUMBER	OUTLOOK	AVERAGE INITIAL SALARY
Bachelor Degrees			
Health Care Officer	168.167-018	Fair	$20,000
Health Services Adviser	187.117-050	Good	18,000
Health Services Worker	070.101-046	Fair	14,000
Health Teacher	091.227-010	Good	18,000
Industrial Hygienist	079.161-010	Fair	28,000
Sanitarian	079.117-010	Fair	19,000
Public Health Educator	079.117-014	Fair	18,000
Public Health Specialist	187.117-050	Good	17,000
Technical Writer	131.267-026	Good/Exc.	19,000
Graduate Degrees			
Health Scientist		Excellent	28,000
Human Performance Researcher		Excellent	30,000
Professor	090.227-010	Good/Exc.	27,000
Sports Psychologist		Good	28,000

HISTORY

History is the study of past civilizations and problems used to promote insight and understanding of the problems of today, preserve our great cultural heritage, and enrich our appreciation of man and his world. History broadens our perspective and allows us to discover the essential elements of human existence. As such, history prepares students for careers in teaching, law, business, government service, advertising, historical editing, and related areas. The surplus of qualified history teachers has limited opportunities in education, but graduates find placement in other occupations.

COURSE REQUIREMENTS

Diplomatic History
Geographical History
Great Historians
Historical Problems
History
Ideas and Man in Modern World
Main Issues in American History

Paleography
The American Heritage
Topics in History
United States History
Writing History
World Civilization

OPTIONS WITHIN MAJOR

Government Agencies
Preparation for Professional School

Teaching

RECOMMENDED HIGH SCHOOL COURSES

English (4 years)
Foreign Language

History

CAREERS	D.O.T. NUMBER	OUTLOOK	AVERAGE INITIAL SALARY
Bachelor Degrees			
Archivist	101.167-010	Fair	$23,000
Biographer	052.067-010	Fair/Poor	Varies
Editor/Journalist	132.037-022	Fair/Good	26,000
Foreign Service Officer	188.117-106	Fair	22,000
Genealogist	052.067-018	Fair/Poor	16,000
Historian	052.067-022	Fair/Poor	21,000
Librarian	100.127-014	Fair/Poor	20,000
Supervisor of Historic Sites		Fair/Poor	19,000
Teacher	091.227-010	Poor	18,000
Graduate Degrees			
Historian	052.067-022	Good	25,000
Historical Society Director	052.067-014	Fair	30,000
Professor	090.227-010	Fair	27,000
Researcher	052.167-010	Good	23,000

HOME ECONOMICS EDUCATION

Home Economics Education prepares students for professional roles in public schools, cooperative extension services, business, or industry. Knowledge and skills obtained in a broad family living program are used to educate individuals and families for better family life, improving goods and services used by families, conducting research, and furthering favorable conditions for optimal family living. The integrated program deals with child development, family finances, economic management, nutritional needs, and interior design and furnishing. Jobs are plentiful and qualified instructors of resource management and homemaking skills easily find employment.

COURSE REQUIREMENTS

Child Development
Curriculum Development
Dress/Pattern Construction
Experiences with Children
Food Science
Home Economics Education
Home Management
Home Nursing
Household Equipment

Human Nutrition
Interior Design
Occupational Home Economics
Education
Psychology of Clothing
Residence Management
Textiles
Textiles for Consumers
The Child in the Family

OPTIONS WITHIN MAJOR

Public Health Specialists

Teaching

RECOMMENDED HIGH SCHOOL COURSES

Art
Biology
Chemistry

English
Homemaking
Speech

CAREERS	D.O.T. NUMBER	OUTLOOK	AVERAGE INITIAL SALARY
Bachelor Degrees			
Extension Service Specialist	096.127-014	Fair	$25,000
Home Economics Teacher	091.227-010	Good	18,000
Home Economist	096.121-014	Fair	19,000
Social Service Worker	195.107-030	Fair/Good	16,000
Graduate Degree			
Professor	090.227-010	Fair	25,000

HORTICULTURE

Horticulture is the science of growing fruits, vegetables, flower, and ornamental plants. The concerns of the horticulturist range from improving the living environment to plant, fruit, and vegetable use and production. Greenhouse and nursery management, landscape design, and other areas of landscaping provide major employment opportunities.

COURSE REQUIREMENTS

Botony
Chemistry
College Algebra
Commercial Fruit Tree Production
Floral Design
Greenhouse Management
Home Landscape and Design
Horticultural Science
Irrigated Soils
Math

Nursery Science
Pest Management
Plant Biology
Plant Growth & Reproduction
Small Fruit Science
Soil Fertility
Soil Science
Turf Science
Weed Science

OPTIONS WITHIN MAJOR

Agri-business
Production

Professional School Preparation

RECOMMENDED HIGH SCHOOL COURSES

Botany
Business
Chemistry

English
Math
Vocational Education

CAREERS	D.O.T. NUMBER	OUTLOOK	AVERAGE INITIAL SALARY
Associate Degrees			
Florist	142.081-010	Good	$12,000
Orchard Grower	403.131-010	Fair	Varies
Bachelor Degrees			
Editor/Writer, Garden Magazine	132.067-018	Fair/Good	23,000
Horticulturist	040.061-038	Fair/Good	19,000
Landscape Architect	001.061-018	Fair/Good	19,000
Landscape Contractor/ Estimator	182.167-014	Good	16,000
Plant Breeder/Inspector	405.361-010	Fair/Good	18,000
Soil Conservationist	040.061-154	Good	17,000
Graduate Degrees			
Plant Pathologist	041.061-082	Good	26,000
Professor	090.227-010	Fair	26,000
Research Horticulturist		Good	26,000

HOTEL MANAGEMENT

Hotel managers are responsible for operating their establishments profitably and satisfying guests. They determine room rates and credit policy, direct the operation of the food service, and manage the housekeeping, accounting, secruity, and maintenance departments of the hotel. Handling problems and coping with the unexpected are important parts of the job.

Most hotels promote employees who have proven their ability, usually as front office clerks, to assistnat managers and eventually to general managers. Employers are, however, increasingly emphasizing college education. A bachelor degree in hotel and restaurant administration provides particularly strong preparation for a career in hotel management.

COURSE REQUIREMENTS

Accounting
Business Administration
Catering
Data Processing
Economics

Food Service Management
Hotel Administration
Hotel Maintenance Engineering
Housekeeping
Tourism

RECOMMENDED HIGH SCHOOL COURSES

Business
English
Foreign Language

Psychology
Public Speaking
Social Studies

CAREERS	D.O.T. NUMBER	OUTLOOK	AVERAGE INITIAL SALARY
Associate Degrees			
Hotel-Motel Clerk	238.362-010	Good	$13,000
Hotel Recreation Manager	187.167-122	Good	19,000
Bachelor Degrees			
Food Services Director	187.167-026	Good	24,000
Hotel & Restaurant Admin.	187.117-038	Good/Exc.	22,000
Hotel & Restaurant Inspector		Fair	19,000

INDUSTRIAL ADMINISTRATION

Physical plant administrators serve in supervisory positions in industry and in the physical plants of school districts, colleges, and universities. Plant Administration involves planning and directing construction of facilities as well as administering maintenance and operations programs once the plant is complete. Expansion in universities and colleges in addition to the many needs of private industry will serve to provide several opportunities in the area of physical plant administration.

COURSE REQUIREMENTS

Building Construction
Chemistry
Economics
Economy, Society, & Public Policy
Elementary Surveying
Engineering Graphics
Field Botany

Fundamental Accounting Policy
Industrial Safety
Manufacturing Processes
Organizational Behavior
Statistics
Technical Math
Undergraduate Seminar

OPTIONS WITH MAJOR

Physical Plant Administration

RECOMMENDED HIGH SCHOOL COURSES

Chemistry
Machine Shop

Math (3 years)
Physics

CAREERS	D.O.T. NUMBER	OUTLOOK	AVERAGE INITIAL SALARY
Bachelor Degrees			
Building Construction Supervisor		Good	$21,000
Construction Inspector	182.267-010	Fair	20,000
Field Supervisor		Good	20,000
Physical Facilities Planner	184.167-210	Fair	21,000
Physical Plant Administrator/ Supervisor	189.117-022	Good	26,000
Plant Engineer	007.161-014	Good	24,000

INDUSTRIAL EDUCATION

Industrial Education prepares graduates for teaching technical or vocational education or industrial arts. An increased emphasis on vocational education and technical skills in various school programs has led to greater opportunites for industrial education teachers. Industrial education teachers who have a broad background in automotives, electronics, graphic arts, metals, plastics, and woods, will have no problem locating a teaching position in a secondary school or a technical college.

COURSE REQUIREMENTS

Adult Industrial Education
Automotive Engines
Career Information/Guidance
Construction Practices
Electricity
Engineering Graphics
Fuel and Electrical Systems
Graphic Arts
Manufacturing
Metalwork Fundamentals

Plastics Processes
Power Sources of Industry
Power Tune-up
Screen Processing
Sheet Metal
Shop Maintenance
Shop Management
Shop Planning
Woodwork Fundamentals

OPTIONS WITHIN MAJOR

Industrial Design

Industrial Education

RECOMMENDED HIGH SCHOOL COURSES

Automotive Shop
Drafting
Electricity

Graphic Arts
Matalwork
Woodwork

CAREERS	D.O.T. NUMBER	OUTLOOK	AVERAGE INITIAL SALARY
Bachelor Degrees			
Industrial Arts Teacher	091.221-010	Good	$18,000
Manual Arts Therapist	076.124-010	Fair	15,000
Technical Teacher	090.227-010	Good	18,000
Vocational Education	097.227-014	Good	18,000
Graduate Degrees			
Administrator	097.167-010	Fair/Good	23,000
Coordinator	099.117-026	Fair/Good	19,000
Professor	090.227-010	Fair/Good	27,000

INFORMATION MANAGEMENT

Many colleges and universities have broadened typical secretarial technology programs to include business education and to take advantage of new computer technologies. In addition to preparation for secretarial opportunities, there is an emphasis on management and office supervision. Job settings are numerous and in a variety of industrial educational, and buiness enterprises.

COURSE REQUIREMENTS

Accounting
Analytical Officer Operations
Business Correspondence
Business Education
Business Machines
Cooperative Business Education
Data Base Information
Economy, Society, and Public Policy
Ergonomics
General College Math
Information Systems Management

Microcomputer Programming
Office Administration
Office Automation
Principles of Statistics
Production Typing
Records Management
Shorthand
Stenographic Procedure
Systems Analysis
Transcription
Typing

OPTIONS WITHIN MAJOR

Data Processing
Office Management

Shorthand
Typing

RECOMMENDED HIGH SCHOOL COURSES

Business
Business Machines
English

Math (3 years)
Shorthand
Typing

CAREERS	D.O.T. NUMBER	OUTLOOK	AVERAGE INITIAL SALARY
Associate Degrees			
Administrative Assistant		Excellent	$22,000
Clerk-Typist	203.362-010	Good	14,000
Data Typist	203.582-022	Good	16,000
Executive Secretary		Excellent	19,000
Legal Secretary	201.362-010	Excellent	16,000
Medical Secretary	201.362-014	Good	16,000
Receptionist		Good	14,000
School Secretary	201.362-022	Poor	14,000
Secretary	201 to 209	Excellent	14,000
Stenographer	202.362-014	Poor	15,000
Terminal Operator	203.362-014	Excellent	14,000
Transcribing Machine Operator	203.582-058	Excellent	14,000
Typist	203.582-066	Excellent	14,000
Word Processing Supervisor	203.132-014	Excellent	19,000

INSURANCE

The insurance industry offers many employment opportunities both for recent high school and college graduates and for experienced workers. About one-half of all insurance employees work in life insurance companies and agencies. Employment of insurance workers is expected to increase faster than the average for all occupations through the 1980's as the insurance industry continues to expand.

COURSE REQUIREMENTS

Comparative Public Financial Security
Employee Benefit Plans
Employee Medical Care
Estate Planning
Financial Security Program
Financing Medical Care
Life & Disability Insurance

Life & Health Insurer Operation
Personal Income Maintenance
Personal Insurance Planning
Problems in Risk & Insurance
Property & Liability Insurance
Property & Liability Operation
Risk Management Insurance

OPTIONS WITHIN MAJOR

Commercial Insurance
Estate Planning

Personal Insurance

RECOMMENDED HIGH SCHOOL COURSES

Biology
Business Law
Math

Public Speaking
Typing

CAREERS	D.O.T. NUMBER	OUTLOOK	AVERAGE INITIAL SALARY
Bachelor Degrees			
Actuary	020.167-010	Good/Exc.	$27,000
Claims Adjuster	241.210-010	Fair/Good	19,000
Claims Examiner	168.267-014	Fair/Good	20,000
Insurance Underwriter	169.167-058	Excellent	19,000
Sales Agent	250.257-010	Excellent	21,000

JAPANESE

With increased importance in interantional commerce, Japan has become a leader in world trade, and students of Japanese find tremendous opportunities in international business and law. Besides business, Japanese is a key language in research in many graduate fields and in the significant study of world history and Asian studies. Five avenues of employment make up the bulk of opportunities for the graduate— government service, business, language research, teaching, and library sciences. Students of Japanese should supplement their language study with geography, comparative literature, and related fields.

COURSE REQUIREMENTS

Compostion
Convertation
Grammar
Japanese

Literature
Phonetics
Translation

OPTIONS WITHIN MAJOR

Business
Education

Translation/Interpretation

RECOMMENDED HIGH SCHOOL COURSES

Foreign Language
Geography
History

Humanities
Literature
Social Science

CAREERS	D.O.T. NUMBER	OUTLOOK	AVERAGE INITIAL SALARY
Bachelor Degrees			
Customs Official	168.267-022	Fair	$16,000
Foreign Service Officer	188.117-106	Fair	22,000
Import/Export Agent	184.117-022	Good	22,000
Inteligence Expert	059.267-010	Good	24,000
Interpreter	137.267-010	Fair/Good	19,000
Language Researcher	059.067-014	Fair	22,000
Public Relations Specialist	165.067-010	Fair/Good	25,000
Scientific Writer		Fair	24,000
Teacher	019.227-010	Poor	18,000
Translator	137.267-018	Good	19,000
Travel Agent	225.157-010	Good	12,000
Graduate Degrees			
Professor	090.227-010	Good	25,000
Scientific Linguist	059.067-014	Fair	24,000

JOURNALISM

Journalism is the profession concerned with gathering, preparing, and communicating information to be presented through newspapers, magazines, trade publications, radio, television, news services, and other types of media. The work performed by journalists includes, reporting, writing, editing, photographing, or broadcasting news items.

COURSE REQUIREMENTS

Advertising
Contemporary Journalism
Feature Writing
History of American Journalism
Industrial Publishing
Mass Communications
Mass Media
Newspaper Editing and Layout
Newswriting

Photojournalism
Public Affairs Reporting
Public Opinion
Public Relations
Radio News
Television News Film
The Law of Mass Media
Typography and Graphic Arts

OPTIONS WITHIN MAJOR

Journalism

Radio/Technician

RECOMMENDED HIGH SCHOOL COURSES

Composition
English Grammar
History

Literature
Math
Public Speaking

CAREERS	D.O.T. NUMBER	OUTLOOK	AVERAGE INITIAL SALARY
Bachelor Degrees			
Columnist	131.067-010	Fair/Good	$19,000
Correspondent	131.267-018	Fair	24,000
Department Editor	132.037-018	Fair	20,000
Journalist	131.267-018	Fair/Good	20,000
Managing Editor	132.017-010	Fair	Varies
News Analyst	131.067-010	Fair	25,000
Newspaper Editor	132.017-014	Fair	24,000
News Editor	132.067-026	Fair	19,000
Radio Newscaster	131.267-010	Fair	18,000
Reporter	131.267-018	Fair/Good	20,000
TV News Boardcaster	249.387-010	Fair	43,000
Graduate Degree			
Professor	090.227-010	Fair	27,000

LANDSCAPE ARCHITECTURE

Landscape architects are hired by many types of organizations from real estate firms starting new developments to municipalities constructing airports or parks. They usually plan the arrangement of vegetation, walkways, and other natural features of open spaces. They may also design areas where constructed materials predominate — as on streets that have been modified to improve pedestrian access and limit automobile traffic. They sometimes supervise the construction stages of outdoor projects.

COURSE REQUIREMENTS

Botany
City Planning
Design Communication
English
Greenhouse Management
Horticulture
Landscape Construction

Mathematics
Nursery Science
Ornamental Horticulture
Science
Sketching
Soil-Plant Relationships
Surveying

RECOMMENDED HIGH SCHOOL COURSES

Art
Botany
English
Graphics

Mathematics (2-3 years)
Mechanical Drawing
Pulbic Speaking

CAREERS	D.O.T. NUMBER	OUTLOOK	AVERAGE INITIAL SALARY
Bachelor Degrees			
Environmental Designer		Fair	$18,000
Landscape Architect	001.061-018	Fair/Good	19,000
Landscape Contractor	182.167-038	Good	16,000

LATIN AMERICAN STUDIES

Latin American Studies is an interdisciplinary program typically referred to as "Area Studies." It integrates ideas and principles from anthropology, literature, history, georgraphy, and economics. This broadly based education allows one to do historical research, social, political, and economic analysis, and literary criticism. Students often continue on to advanced studies in law, business administration, and liberal arts, or may become involved in teaching or government service.

COURSE REQUIREMENTS

Archaeology of South America
Business and Culture
Central American Society
Colonization of Latin America
Comparative Governments
Economic Development
History of Argentina
History of Brazil
History of Chile

History of Mexico
Inter-American Relations
International Relations
Latin American Geography
Latin American Politics
Mesoamerican Archaeology
Mesoamerican History
Social Anthropology
Social Change in Latin America

OPTIONS WITHIN MAJOR

Archaeology/Anthropology
Business
Humanities

International Politics
Politics

RECOMMENDED HIGH SCHOOL COURSES

Art
Economics
English
Foreign Language

Geography
History
Literature

CAREERS	D.O.T. NUMBER	OUTLOOK	AVERAGE INITIAL SALARY
Bachelor Degrees			
Biographer	052.067-010	Fair/Poor	Varies
Correspondent	131.267-018	Fair	$23,000
Foreign Service Officer	188.117-106	Fair	22,000
Historian	052.067-022	Fair/Poor	21,000
Import/Export Agent	184.117-022	Good	22,000
Intelligence Expert	059.267-010	Good	26,000
Public Relations Specialist	165.067-010	Fair	25,000
Publications Editor	132.037-026	Poor	20,000
Travel Agent	225.157-010	Good	14,000
Graduate Degrees			
Foreign Service	051.067-010	Good	27,000
Professor	090.227-010	Good	27,000
Researcher	052.167-010	Good	25,000

LAW

Every major industry, institution, and organization, as well as every individual citizen is affected by the law to some degree. As a result, lawyers enter many careers and occupational opportunities. Approximately three-fourths of all the lawyers in the United States are in private practice, and the government employs the greatest number of salaried attorneys. A background in law also allows graduates opportunities in business (especially insurance firms), education, and politics. Although competition to enter law school is keen, the job market is wide open for those who complete the program.

COURSE REQUIREMENTS

General courses are emphasized on the Bachelor Degree or Pre-law level with the following suggested areas:

English	Political Science
History	Psychology
Humanities	Speech

Graduate Studies cover many aspects of law including:

Accounting	Negotiations
Anti-trust	Oil & Gas
Civil Procedure	Public Land
Criminal	Regulative
Industries	Securities
Jurisprudence	State & Local Government
Labor	Trade Regulations
Legislation	Wills and Estates

RECOMMENDED HIGH SCHOOL COURSES

English	Math
History	Writing

CAREERS	D.O.T. NUMBER	OUTLOOK	AVERAGE INITIAL SALARY
Graduate Degrees			
Bar Examiner	110.167-010	Fair/Good	$37,000
Business Consultant-Administrator	199.251-010	Excellent	Varies
Criminal Lawyer	110.107-014	Good	36,000
Corporate Lawyer	110.117-022	Excellent	34,000
District Attorney	110.117-010	Fair/Good	38,000
Insurance Lawyer	110.117-014	Good/Exc.	31,000
Judge	111.117-010	Fair/Good	60,000
Lawyer	110.107-010	Excellent	33,000
Patent Lawyer	110.117-026	Good	36,000
Probate Lawyer	110.117-030	Excellent	33,000
Professor	090.227-010	Good	36,000
Real Estate Lawyer	110.117-034	Good	30,000
Tax Attorney	110.117-038	Excellent	32,000
Title Attorney	110.117-042	Good	30,000

LIBRARY SCIENCE

Library work is divided into two areas: User Services and Technical Services. Librarians in user services work directly with the public helping them find the information they need. Technical services librarians are primarily concerned with acquiring and preapring materials for use and deal less frequently with the public. Employment opportunities are available in schools, public libraries, private industry, government agencies, hospitals, correctional facitlites, consultants or as faculty in schools of library science.

COURSE REQUIREMENTS

Acquisition of Materials
Administration
Archives and Manuscripts
Cataloging & Classification
Government Publications
Infomation Retrieval

Information Systems
Manuscription
Media Center
Organization of Materials
Reference Theory
Research Services

OPTIONS WITHIN MAJOR

Research

Technical Services

RECOMMENDED HIGH SCHOOL COURSES

Art
English
History

Literature
Science

CAREERS	D.O.T. NUMBER	OUTLOOK	AVERAGE INITIAL SALARY
Associate Degree			
Library Technician	100.367-018	Good	$13,000
Bachelor Degrees			
Archivist	101.167-010	Fair	23,000
Audio Visual Librarian	100.167-010	Fair	15,000
Cataloger	100.387-010	Fair/Poor	14,000
Classifier	100.367-014	Fair/Poor	17,000
Librarian	100.127-014	Good	20,000
Media Specialist	100.167-030	Fair	15,000
Public Librarian	100.127-014	Good	16,000
Reference Librarian		Fair	17,000
School Librarian		Good	15,000
Graduate Degrees			
Acquisition Librarian	100.267-010	Fair	26,000
Professor	090.227-010	Good	26,000
Special Collections	100.267-014	Fair	25,000

LINGUISTICS

With the world sharing more in terms of industry, education, medicine, and science and technology, communications among the countries of the world becomes increasingly important. Technological advancements such as computer translation allows students to study in the more traditional track or specialize in training with computer applications to language. Different from the study of foreign language, linguistics studies the structure and application of language in general.

COURSE REQUIREMENTS

Comparative Linguistics
German
History of English Language
History of Language
Humanities Computing
Junction Grammar
Language Acquisition
Language and Culture
Language and Computers
Latin
Modern Linguistics

Philosophy
Phonology
Psychology and Language
Set Theory Mathematics
Semantics
Spanish
Speech Processing
Syntactic Theory
Translation
Uncommon Languages

OPTIONS WITHIN MAJOR

Business
Computer Translation

International Consulting
Research

RECOMMENDED HIGH SCHOOL COURSES

Computer Science
English (3 years)
Foreign Language

History
Math (3 years)

CAREERS	D.O.T. NUMBER	OUTLOOK	AVERAGE INITIAL SALARY
Bachelor Degrees			
English as Second Language Instructor		Good	$18,000
Intelligence Expert	059.267-010	Good	24,000
Translator	137.267-018	Good	19,000
Graduate Degrees			
Computer Translator		Excellent	35,000
Professor	090.227-010	Good	28,000
Researcher		Excellent	27,000
Scientific Linguist	059.067-014	Fair	25,000

MANUFACTURING ENGINEERING TECHNOLOGY

As a chief industry in the United States, manufacturing employs over 19 million people who account for over 25% of the dollars earned. Manufacturing technology combines engineering and management principles and skills for planning, developing, implementing, and controlling industrial manufacturing processes. The manufacturing technologist analyzes and plans process equipment and facilities required for the fabrication and assembly of products. Increased sophistication of manufacturing with computer-aided techniques has greatly increased the international job market for qualified graduates.

COURSE REQUIREMENTS

Advanced Mechanical Drafting
Applied Mechanics
Applied Physics
Basic Fluid Power
Computer-aided Graphics
Computer-aided Manufacturing
Computer Programming
Cost Metal Processes
Economy, Society, &
   Public Policy
Electrical Machines and
   Controls
Industrial Electronics
Industrial Robotics
Machine Tool Performance
Manufacturing
Manufacturing Development

Manufacturing Practicum
Manufacturing Process Planning
Manufacturing Processes
Mechanical Drafting
Metal Forming
Numerical Control Programming
Plastic Tooling Processing
Physical Metallurgy
Production Operations
Production Planning
Quality Assurance
Scientific Computing
Technical Mathematics
Technical Writing
Tool Design
Welding Processes

OPTIONS WITHIN MAJOR

Automated Systems
Computer-integrated Manufacturing
Management

Manufacturing
Welding

139

RECOMMENDED HIGH SCHOOL COURSES

Algebra   Physics
Algebra II   Trigonometry
Drafting   Woodworking
Machine Shop

CAREERS	D.O.T. NUMBER	OUTLOOK	AVERAGE INITIAL SALARY
Associate Degrees			
Industrial Laboratory Technician		Excellent	$19,000
Materials Science Technician	029.081-014	Good	15,000
Bachelor Degrees			
Die Designer	007.161-010	Good	21,000
Industrial Engineer	012.167-030	Excellent	28,000
Manufacturing Engineer	012.167-042	Excellent	27,000
Process Engineer		Excellent	24,000
Project Engineer	019.167-014	Excellent	24,000
Quality Control Engineer	012.167-054	Excellent	27,000
Tool Designer	007.061-022	Good	25,000
Tool Programmer	007.167-018	Good	26,000
Graduate Degrees			
Computer-aided Mfg. Consultant		Excellent	30,000
Professor	090.227-010	Excellent	28,000

MARKETING AND RETAILING

Marketing and retailing are necessary in an economy based on business transaction. As the world is more easily traversed regarding international business, this major increases in both impact and complexity. Graduates from this major find themselves contribuiting in retail management, industrial marketing, sales management, forecasting and market research, personnel, merchandising, financial control, and store operations.

COURSE REQUIREMENTS

Accounting
Business Policy
Buying Behavior
Financial Management
Information Management
International Marketing
Management Economics
Market Analysis and Forecasting

Marketing Management
Marketing Models
Marketing Research
Operations Management
Organizational Behavior
Promotion Management
Retail Management
Sales and Distribution

OPTIONS WITHIN MAJOR

Marketing
International Business

Retailing

RECOMMENDED HIGH SCHOOL COURSES

Algebra
English

Geometry
History

CAREERS	D.O.T. NUMBER	OUTLOOK	AVERAGE INITIAL SALARY
Bachelor Degrees			
Buyer	162.157-018	Fair/Good	$22,000
Job Analyst	166.267-018	Good/Exc.	19,000
Market Research Analyst	050.067-014	Good/Exc.	24,000
Personnel Manager	166.117-018	Excellent	30,000
Purchasing Agent	162.157-038	Good	24,000
Retail Manager	185.117-167	Good/Exc.	22,000
Sales Manager	165.167-018	Good	23,000
Graduate Degrees			
Marketing Retail Analyst	050.067-014	Excellent	29,000
Professor	090.227-010	Good	29,000

MATHEMATICS

Mathematics is a precise academic discipline which defies simplistic definition. It is a fundamental tool in education, government, and almost every other profession or area of study. Elements of language, art, and science are aspects of math that prepare students for work in business and industry, as well as in specialized areas of mathematics. Approximately 58 percent of all professional mathematicians work in management or administration. Many graduates also pursue other professional or advanced degree studies.

COURSE REQUIREMENTS

Abstract Algebra
Calculus and Analysis
Calculus of Several Variable
Complex Analysis
Differential Equations
Finite Mathematics
Graph Theory
History of Mathematics

Linear Algebra
Matrix Analysis
Numerical Analysis
Numerical Methods Technology
Real Analysis
Set Theory
Theory of Numbers

OPTIONS WITHIN MAJOR

Computational Mathematics
Mathematics

Mathematics Science
Mathematics Philosophy

RECOMMENDED HIGH SCHOOL COURSES

Algebra (2 years)
Calculus
Chemistry
Geometry

Foreign Language
Physics
Trigonometry

CAREERS	D.O.T. NUMBER	OUTLOOK	AVERAGE INITIAL SALARY
Bachelor Degrees			
Actuary	020.167-010	Good	$27,000
Auditor	160.162-014	Good/Exc.	25,000
Efficiency Engineer	012.167-070	Fair	22,000
Mathematician	020.067-014	Good	29,000
Navigator	196.167-014	Fair	24,000
Operations Research Analyst	020.067-018	Good	26,000
Psychometrician	045.067-018	Good	26,000
Teacher	091.227-010	Good	18,000
Graduate Degrees			
Auditor	160.162-014	Excellent	29,000
Computer Applications Engineer	020.062-010	Excellent	32,000
Professor	090.227-010	Good	27,000
Statistician	620.067-022	Excellent	27,000
Theoretical Mathematician		Excellent	33,000

MECHANICAL ENGINEERING

Mechanical engineering is the applied science that deals with analysis, design, development, fabrication, and application of products that are predominately mechanical and energy related. The field includes many varieties of specialization from farm machinery to consumer goods (such as automobiles, equipment, etc.). Projected needs in the area of mechanical engineering exceed the number of graduates expected, and job opportunities should remain plentiful in the near future.

COURSE REQUIREMENTS

Aerospace
Analytical Geometry and Calculus
Applied Metallurgy
Applied Ordinary Differential
  Equations
Automatic Controls
Bioengineering
College Chemistry
Design for Manufacture Areas
Electrical Engineering
Engineering Graphics
Engineering Mechanics
Fluid Mechanics
Heat Transfer

Kinematics
Manufacture of Machine
Components
Mechanical Design
Mechanical Engineering
Instrumentation
Metallurgy
Nuclear Engineering
Numerical Methods
Physics
Solid Mechanic
System Design
Thermodynamics
Vibrations and Dynamics

OPTIONS WITHIN MAJOR

Aerospace
Automatic Controls Systems Analysis
Bioengineering
Fluid Mechanics

Heat Transfer
Materials and Metallurgy
Thermodynamics

RECOMMENDED HIGH SCHOOL COURSES

Chemistry   Mechanical Drawing
English (4 years)   Physics
Math (3 years)

CAREERS	D.O.T. NUMBER	OUTLOOK	AVERAGE INITIAL SALARY
Bachelor Degrees			
Automotive Engineer	007.061-010	Good	$25,000
Construction Supervisor		Good/Exc.	24,000
Design Engineer	007.061-018	Good	26,000
Industrial Designer	142.061-026	Good/Exc.	22,000
Mechanical Engineer	007.061-014	Excellent	27,000
Plant Manager	183.117-010	Good	26,000
Graduate Degrees			
Engineer	007.061-014	Excellent	35,000
Engineering Researcher	024.167-010	Good/Exc.	35,000
University Professor	090.227-010	Good/Exc.	30,000

MEDICAL TECHNOLOGY

Medical technology graduates are prepared in laboratory procedures to assist in the examination and treatment of patients. Some medical technologists do research in laboratory technique or drug exploration, but more than 80% perform tests in microbiology, parasitology, biochemistry, blood banking, hematology, histology, or nuclear medical technology in the hospital setting where opportunities are excellent.

COURSE REQUIREMENTS

Biochemistry
Biology
Botany
Chemistry
College Algebra
Epidemology
Human Parasitology
Immunology

Medical Technology
Microbiology
Organic Chemistry
Pathogenic Microbiology
Pathophysiology
Physics
Zoology

OPTIONS WITHIN MAJOR

Institutional Care

Laboratory Science

RECOMMENDED HIGH SCHOOL COURSES

Biology
Chemistry
English (4 years)

Math (3 years)
Physics

CAREERS	D.O.T. NUMBER	OUTLOOK	AVERAGE INITIAL SALARY
Associate Degrees			
Dental Technologist	078.361-010	Excellent	$14,000
Dialysis Technician	078.362-014	Good	18,000
Electrocardiographic Technician	078.362-018	Good/Exc.	15,000
Electroencephalographic Technician	078.362-022	Good/Exc.	15,000
Medical Laboratory Technician	078.381-014	Excellent	18,000
Radiological Technologist	078.362-026	Excellent	19,000
Respiratory Therapist	078.361-010	Good/Exc.	22,000
Tissue Technologist	078.361-030	Good	16,000
Ultra Sound Technologist	078.364-010	Good	22,000
X-ray Technician	078.362-026	Good/Exc.	14,000
Bachelor Degrees			
Cytotechnologist	078.261-018	Fair	18,000
Hospital or Health Service Coordinator		Excellent	23,000
Medical Technologist	078.361-014	Excellent	22,000
Nuclear Medical Technologist	078.361-010	Good	21,000
Orthotist	078.261-018	Good	20,000
Pharmaceutical Salesman	262.157-010	Good	25,000
Prosthetist	078.261-022	Good	19,000
Graduate Degrees			
Hospital Laboratory Education Administrator	187.117-010	Excellent	23,000
Medical Researcher		Excellent	32,000
Professor	090.227-010	Good	27,000

MEDICINE

Despite a growing need for medical services, present medical schools' limited capacities make competition for entrance into the medical field very keen. Only students who score very well on the Medical Schools' Admission Test and maintain outstanding grade-point averages are considered for admission. Although the exact sciences are satisfactory in preparing the undergraduate, more and more students are selecting preporfessional majors that can serve as alternates to medical school if they are not selected. Students should pursue a broad general education in addition to the extensive science prerequisites to enhance their possibilities for acceptance into medical schools.

COURSE REQUIREMENTS

Most students accepted to medical school have a bachelor degree. Courses include the following:

Anatomy	Physiology
Biochemistry	Psychology
Chemistry	Qualitative Analysis
Genetics	Quantitative Analysis
Microbiology	Vertebrate Anatomy
Physics	

Professional school courses are a continuation of those above in more depth and with clinical experience.

RECOMMENDED HIGH SCHOOL COURSES

Biology	Math (3 years)
Chemistry	Physics
English (4 years)	Physiology

CAREERS	D.O.T. NUMBER	OUTLOOK	AVERAGE INITIAL SALARY
Graduate Degrees			
Acupuncturist	079.271-010	Excellent	$ 55,000
Allergist	070.107-010	Excellent	95,000
Anesthesiologist	070.101-010	Excellent	110,000
Cardiologist	070.101-014	Excellent	108,000
Dermatologist	070.101-018	Excellent	95,000
Family Practitioner	070.101-026	Excellent	90,000
General Practitioner	070.101-022	Excellent	90,000
Gynecologist	070.101-034	Excellent	100,000
Internist	070.101-042	Excellent	108,000
Neurologist	070.101-050	Excellent	110,000
Obstetrician	070.101-054	Excellent	100,000
Opthalmologist	070.101-058	Excellent	95,000
Orthopedic Surgeon	070.101-	Excellent	100,000
Pathologist	070.061-010	Excellent	105,000
Pediatrician	070.101-066	Excellent	85,000
Proctologist	070.101-086	Excellent	95,000
Psychiatrist	070.107-014	Excellent	95,000
Radiologist	070.101-090	Excellent	95,000
Surgeon	070.101-094	Excellent	110,000
Urologist	070.101-098	Excellent	100,000

METALLURGICAL ENGINEERING

Metallurgical engineers develop new types of metal with characteristics that are tailored to meet specific requirements, such as heat resistance, high strength but lightweight, or high malleability. They also develop methods to process and convert metals into useful products.

The metalworking industries — primarily the iron and steel and nonferrous metals industries, employ over one-half the metallurgical and materials engineers. Metallurgical engineers also work in industries that manufacture machinery, electrical equipment, aircraft parts, and in the mining industries. Some work for government agencies, colleges and universities.

COURSE REQUIREMENTS

Algebra
Calculus & Analytic Geometry
Chemistry
Computer Programming
Engineering Communications
Engineering Mechanics

Materials Science
Statistical Methods
Systems Methodology
Thermal-Fluid Phenomena
Trigonometry
Physics

OPTIONS WITH MAJOR

Chemical Metallurgy

Physical Metallurgy

RECOMMENDED HIGH SCHOOL COURSES

Chemistry
Drafting
English

Math (3 years)
Physics

CAREERS	D.O.T. NUMBER	OUTLOOK	AVERAGE INITIAL SALARY
Associate Degrees			
Metal/Materials Technician	011.261-010	Excellent	$17,000
Metallurgical Engineering Technician	011.061-010	Excellent	18,000
Bachelor Degrees			
Chemical Metallurgist		Excellent	26,000
Extractive Metallurgist	011.061-018	Good	21,000
Metallographer	011.001-014	Excellent	23,000
Physical Metallurgist	011.061-022	Excellent	29,000
Graduate Degree			
Professor	090.227-010	Excellent	27,000

MICROBIOLOGY

Microbiology is the study of microscopic forms of life (bacteria, viruses, molds, yeasts, algae, protozoa) used in food and industrial microbiology, immunology, medical microbiologist, microbial ecology and genetics microbial physiology, and virology. Preprofessional students (medical and dental) find microbiology excellent training for their graduate work. Employment opportunities are available in industry, hospitals, government agencies, and universities.

COURSE REQUIREMENTS

Algebra
Bacterial Physiology
Biochemistry
Biology
Chemical Pathology
Chemistry
Epidemiology
Food & Dairy Microbiology
Genetics
Immunology

Microbial Genetics
Microbiology
Organic Chemistry
Pathogenic Microbiology
Pathophysiology
Physics
Statistics
Trigonometry
Virology
Water & Sewage Microbiology

OPTIONS WITHIN MAJOR

Environmental Health Science

Laboratory Services

RECOMMENDED HIGH SCHOOL COURSES

Biology
Chemistry
English

Math (3 years)
Physics

CAREERS	D.O.T. NUMBER	OUTLOOK	AVERAGE INITIAL SALARY
Bachelor Degrees			
Cytotechnologist	078.281-010	Good	$18,000
Environmental Health Scientist	029.261-014	Good	17,000
Microbiologist	041.061-058	Good	22,000
Public Health Scientist	041.261-010	Good	19,000
Quality Control Lab Technician	012.261-014	Good	17,000
Microbiology Technologist	678.261-014	Good/Exc.	19,000
Graduate Degrees			
Cytologist	041.061-042	Good	25,000
Parasitologist	041.061-070	Good	26,000
Professor	090.227-010	Good	27,000
Researcher		Excellent	29,000

MINING AND GEOLOGICAL ENGINEERING

The mining (mineral) engineer works with mineral deposits of all kinds from the time of their discovery through their evaluation and production. Although his chief job is ususally to get the most ore out of the ground for the least cost, the mining engineer often works in many other areas, such as research, safety, design, environment, pollution control, and management.

Major metal, mining, and coal companies are leading prospects for jobs for mineral engineers who have strong career convictions and an eye toward possible advancement to management positions. Power and steel companies often own subsidiary companies that also employ mineral engineers. Manufacturers dealing with fertilizers, mining machinery, and equipment are good job opportunities, as are cement companies and quarries of various types.

COURSE REQUIREMENTS

Bulk Materials Handling
Calculus
Drilling and Blasting
Electrical Circuits
Engineering Physics
Environmental Engineering
Fluid Mechanics
Materials Testing
Mechanics of Materials

Metallurgy for Engineers
Mineral Exploitation
Mineralogy
Mining Computations
Petrology
Rock Mechanics
Structural Geology
Surveying

OPTIONS WITHIN MAJOR

Fluid Mechanics
Geology

Mining Engineering

RECOMMENDED HIGH SCHOOL COURSES

Algebra	Mechanical Drawing
Chemistry	Trigonometry
Geography	Physics
Geometry	

CAREERS	D.O.T. NUMBER	OUTLOOK	AVERAGE INITIAL SALARY
Associate Degree			
Mining Engineer Technician		Good	$15,000
Bachelor Degrees			
Coal Petroleum Engineer	010.161-018	Excellent	33,000
Mining Engineer	010.061-014	Excellent	25,000
Mining Geologist	024.061-022	Excellent	27,000
Graduate Degrees			
Professor	090.227-010	Excellent	28,000
Researcher	101.161-010	Excellent	31,000

MUSIC

Music includes the study of theory, composition, arrangement, teaching, and performance. Graduates may pursue careers as skilled performers in the concert or professional world, as music teachers in elementary or secondary schools, or on a private basis. Teaching opportunities are still good in many areas but arranging, composing, directing, and conducting openings are very limited.

COURSE REQUIREMENTS

Analytical Techniques
Essentials of Conducting
History of Music
Music Theory
Pedagogy

Performance Instruction
Private Instruction
Recital
Survey Music Literature

OPTIONS WITHIN MAJOR

Composition
Education
Music Theory

Performance
Piano Technician

RECOMMENDED HIGH SCHOOL COURSES

Band
Choral
Music Composition

Music Theory
Private Lessons

CAREERS	D.O.T. NUMBER	OUTLOOK	AVERAGE INITIAL SALARY
Associate Degree			
Piano Technician	730.281-038	Good	$12,000
Bachelor Degrees			
Arranger	152.067-010	Poor	20,000
Composer	152.067-014	Poor	28,000
Music Therapist	076.127-014	Fair	15,000
Music Director, Instructor	152.047-010	Fair/Good	26,000
Music Director, TV	152.047-018	Fair/Good	20,000
Music Copyist	152.267-010	Fair/Good	20,000
Performer	152.041-010	Fair/Good	Varies
Teacher	152.021-010	Good	18,000
Graduate Degree			
Professor	090.227-010	Excellent	26,000

NEAR EASTERN STUDIES

Near Eastern Studies is an interdisciplinary program typically referred to as "Area Studies." It integrates ideas and principles from anthropology, literature, history, geography, and economics. This broadly based education allows one to do historical research, social, political, and economic analysis, and literary criticism. Students often continue on to advanced studies in law, business administration, and liberal arts, or may become involved in teaching or government service.

COURSE REQUIREMENTS

Ancient Egypt and Mesopotamia
Arab-Israeli Conflict
Asiatic Russia
Biblical Archaeology
Geography of the Near East
Humanities of the Islamic World
Humanities of the Near East

Islamic Philosophy and Religion
Jewish Philosophy and Religion
Near Eastern Archaeology
Near Eastern History
Peoples of the Middle East
Political Systems
Studies in Ancient Languages

OPTIONS WITHIN MAJOR

International Politics

Religion/Philosophy

RECOMMENDED HIGH SCHOOL COURSES

Art
Economics
English
Foreign Language

Geography
History
Literature

CAREERS	D.O.T. NUMBER	OUTLOOK	AVERAGE INITIAL SALARY
Bachelor Degrees			
Biographer	052.067-010	Fair/Poor	Varies
Correspondent	131.267-018	Fair	$23,000
Foreign Service Officer	188.117-106	Fair	22,000
Historian	052.067-022	Fair/Poor	21,000
Import/Export Agent	184.117-022	Good	22,000
Intellignece Expert	059.267-010	Good	24,000
Public Relations Specialist	165.067-010	Fair	25,000
Publications Editor	132.037-026	Poor	20,000
Travel Agent	225.157-010	Good	14,000
Graduate Degrees			
Foreign Service	051.067-010	Good	29,000
Professor	090.227-010	Good	29,000
Researcher	052.167-010	Good	25,000

NURSING

Nurses are constantly in demand as an integral part of the health service professions. Hospitals, clinics, public health agencies, armed services, schools, and comprehensive mental health centers find the skills and assistance of qualified nurses indispensable. Besides a need for undergraduate nurses, there is a great demand for nurses with advanced education as clinicians, specialists, researchers, teachers, and administrators. Excellent employment service opportunities exist for men and women throughout the nation and in foreign countries as well.

COURSE REQUIREMENTS

Biophysical assessment
Chemistry
Child Development
Clinical Care
College Algebra
Community Health
Emergency
Essentials in Nutrition
Family Health Management
Human Anatomy
Intensive Care
Medical-surgical
Microbiology
Obstetrics
Pathology
Patient Relationships
Pharmacology
Preceptorship
Primary Care
Psychiatric Nursing
Psychology
Psychosocial Nursing
Research
Social Psychology

OPTIONS WITHIN MAJOR

Clinical Nursing
Institutional Nursing
Nursing Administration

RECOMMENDED HIGH SCHOOL COURSES

Algebra
Biology
Chemistry
English
Geometry
Physics
Physiology
Psychology

CAREERS	D.O.T. NUMBER	OUTLOOK	AVERAGE INITIAL SALARY
Associate Degree			
Licensed Practical Nurse	079.374-014	Excellent	$15,000
Bachelor Degrees			
Industrial Nurse	075.117-020	Excellent	22,000
Nurse Anesthetist	075.371-010	Excellent	35,000
Nurse Instructor	075.121-010	Excellent	24,000
Nurse Midwife	075.264-014	Good	26,000
Primary Care Practitioner	075.264-010	Excellent	25,000
Public Health Nurse	075.117-014	Good	17,000
Registered Nurse	075.374-010	Excellent	24,000
Graduate Degrees			
Nursing/Supervisor	075.127-022	Excellent	28,000
Professor	075.121-010	Excellent	27,000

OCCUPATIONAL HEALTH AND SAFETY

Occupational health and safety is involved with the techniques of recognizing, evaluation, and controlling health and safety hazards in industry. Specific hazard areas of radiation, toxic gases, fumes, dusts, noise ergonomics, and safety are the concern of the occupational hygienist. Employment opportunities are excellent within various industries and public health agencies.

COURSE REQUIREMENTS

Computer Science
Epidemiology
Human Physiology
Leadership Development
Occupational Health Instrumentation

Occupational/Industrial Health
Organic Chemistry
Organizational Behavior
Physics
Safety Education

OPTIONS WITHIN MAJOR

Industrial Health & Safety

Occupational Health & Safety

RECOMMENDED HIGH SCHOOL COURSES

Chemistry
Biology
Physiology

English
Math

CAREERS	D.O.T. NUMBER	OUTLOOK	AVERAGE INITIAL SALARY
Bachelor Degrees			
Environmental Health Specialist	029.261-014	Good	$17,000
Industrial Hygienist	079.161-010	Good/Exc.	28,000
Industrial Health Engr.	012.167-034	Good	25,000
Occupational Safety Inspector	168.167-062	Good/Exc.	22,000
Safety Manager	012.167-058	Good	23,000

OCCUPATIONAL THERAPY

Occupational therapists assist people in special situations prepare themselves for job entry. Handicapped students are assisted by career assessments followed by placement programs. Other settings for this career are mental health agencies and hospitals.

COURSE REQUIREMENTS

Career Assessment
Career Counseling
Correctional Physical Education
Counseling
Group Dynamics
Heredity
Human Growth & Development

Job Placement
Psychometrics
Psychosocial Dysfunctions
Special Education
Statistics
Technical Writing
Work Evaluation

Often a bachelor degree is needed to apply for the competitive acceptance into professional (graduate) school.

OPTIONS WITHIN MAJOR

Physical Therapy

RECOMMENDED HIGH SCHOOL COURSES

English
Math   (2 years)

Sociology

CAREERS	D.O.T. NUMBER	OUTLOOK	AVERAGE INITIAL SALARY
Bachelor Degrees			
Occupational Therapist	076.121-010	Excellent	$22,000
Counselor	045.107-010	Excellent	23,000

OCEANOGRAPHY

Oceanographers use the principles and techniques of natural science, mathematics, and engineering to study oceans—their movements, physical properties, and plant and animal life. Their research not only extends basic scientific knowledge, but also helps develop practical methods for forecasting weather, developing fisheries, mining ocean resources, and improving national defense. Oceanographers find job opportunities available in colleges and universities, and in the Federal Government. Federal agencies employing substantial numbers of oceanographers include the Navy and the National Oceanic and Atmospheric Administration. Some oceanographers work in private industry, and a few work for fishery laboratories of state and local governments.

COURSE REQUIREMENTS

Biological Oceanography
Chemical Oceanography
Chemistry
Geology
Geophysics
Life Support & Diving Technology

Meteorology
Ocean Engineering
Ocean Measurements
Oceanography
Physical Oceanography
Physics

OPTIONS WITHIN MAJOR

Biological Oceanography
Chemical Oceanography

Geological Oceanography
Physical Oceanography

RECOMMENDED HIGH SCHOOL COURSES

Biology
Chemistry
English

Math (3 years)
Physics
Physiology

CAREERS	D.O.T. NUMBER	OUTLOOK	AVERAGE INITIAL SALARY
Bachelor Degree			
Marine Biologist	041.061-022	Good	$18,000
Graduate Degrees			
Geographer	029.067-010	Good	27,000
Marine Geologist	024.061-018	Excellent	25,000
Oceanographic Engineer		Fair/Poor	25,000
Physical Geographer	029.067-014	Good	27,000
Physical Oceanographer	024.061-030	Good	25,000
Professor	090.227-010	Good	27,000

OPTOMETRY

An optometrist assists people with visual defects to see efficiently by making tests and prescribing visual aids (which do not require drugs or surgery). Eighty per cent of the optometrists in the United States are self-employed. Employment opportunities continue to grow as the population's eye care needs increase. Students' grade-point average is of prime importance in consideration for graduate school.

COURSE REQUIREMENTS

There are thirteen optometry schools in the United States and Canada requiring course work in the following in order to be accepted:

Anatomy   Psychology
Biochemistry   Physics
Chemistry   Physiology
English   Vertebrate Anatomy
Math   Zoology
Microbiology

RECOMMENDED HIGH SCHOOL COURSES

Algebra   Geometry
Chemistry   Physics
English   Physiology

CAREERS	D.O.T. NUMBER	OUTLOOK	AVERAGE INITIAL SALARY
Graduate Degree			
Optometrist	079.101-018	Excellent	$30,000

PHARMACY

Pharmacy is a health profession dealing with the preparation and distribution of drugs and medicines prescribed by practitioners. Besides knowing the chemistry of compounds and their effects on human beings, a pharmacist is generally required to understand sound business management and personnel supervision. Large pharmaceutical firms and drugstores make up the majority of job opportunities in this field.

COURSE REQUIREMENTS

Three to four years of undergraduate programs are needed to enter professional school. Undergraduate courses include:

Algebra	Math
Anatomy	Microbiology
Biochemistry	Physics
Chemistry	Physiology
English	

Professional schools require different courses for entrance. They continue the same types of courses but are more specialized and detailed.

RECOMMENDED HIGH SCHOOL COURSES

Algebra	English
Biology	Geometry
Chemistry	Physiology

CAREERS	D.O.T. NUMBER	OUTLOOK	AVERAGE INITIAL SALARY
Graduate Degree			
Pharmacist	074.161-010	Good	$32,000

PHILOSOPHY

Philosophy fosters creative and critical thinking and helps one to understand human thought through the ages. Students often major in another discipline at the same time they are studying philosophy. This joint major program is excellent preparation for law and for other preprofessional programs.

COURSE REQUIREMENTS

Aesthetics
Ancient and Medieval Originals
   of Western Philosophy
Directed Readings in Philosophy
Epistemology
Ethics
Evaluation Arguments and Evidence
Figures in Philosophy
Foundations of Philosophical
   Thought

Graduate Seminar
Intermediate Logic
Logic and Language
Metaphysics
Philosophy of Religion
Readings in Philosophy
The Emergence of Modern
Philosophy
Topics in Philosophy

RECOMMENDED HIGH SCHOOL COURSES

English
Forensics
Languages

Mathematics
Philosophy

CAREERS	D.O.T. NUMBER	OUTLOOK	AVERAGE INITIAL SALARY
Bachelor Degrees			
Clergy	120.007-010	Good	$23,000
Editorial Writer	131.067-022	Fair	23,000
Intelligence Expert	059.267-010	Good	24,000
Graduate Degrees			
Critic	131.067-018	Fair	30,000
Professor	090.227-010	Poor	27,000

PHYSICAL EDUCATION

An increasing emphasis on physical fitness throughout the country has opened new opportunities for physical education graduates as athletic directors in sports clubs, exercise specialists in health clubs, and athletic trainers in amateur and professional teams. Still, the major source of employment is teaching and coaching in public and private schools and universities with many and varied opportunities in sports and dance. Several students continue on in graduate work to do research or become administrators of various athletic interests.

COURSE REQUIREMENTS

Adaptive & Corrective Physical
   Education
Advanced Life Saving
Child Development
Diagnosis of Athletic Injuries
Human Anatomy
Human Physiology

Motor Learning
Physical Education
Physical Education for Teachers
Sports Fundamentals
Statistics

OPTIONS WITHIN MAJOR

Athletic Training
Coaching
Elementary Education

Intramural Sports
Secondary Education
Special Education

RECOMMENDED HIGH SCHOOL COURSES

Biology
Extramural Sports
Intramural Sports

Math
Physiology

CAREERS	D.O.T. NUMBER	OUTLOOK	AVERAGE INITIAL SALARY
Bachelor Degrees			
Athletic Manager, College	153.117-014	Poor	$22,000
Athletic Trainer	153.224-010	Good/Exc.	16,000
Coach, High School	153.227-010	Fair/Good	22,000
Exercise Specialist		Good/Fair	16,000
Physical Education Teacher	091.227-010	Fair/Good	18,000
Recreation Director	187.137-010	Good	15,000
Graduate Degrees			
Athletic Director		Fair	25,000
Exercise Physiologist		Excellent	35,000
Sports Psychologist		Fair/Good	28,000
Intramural Sports Director		Fair	22,000
Professor	090.227-010	Fair/Good	26,000
Researcher		Good	27,000

PHYSICAL THERAPY

Physical Therapists work with disabled individuals who suffer handicaps from illness, accident, or birth. The therapist evaluates neuromuscular, musculo-skeletal, sensorimotor, and related cardiovascular and respiratory functions of the patient. Besides evaluation, the therapist supervises activities to increase muscle strength, motor development, functional capacity, circulatory and respiratory efficiency. The preprofessional program prepares students to enter professional schools in their respective interests. Job opportunities are excellent in hospitals, clinics, or private practice.

COURSE REQUIREMENTS

Body Responses to Health and Disease
Chemistry
Health of the Body Systems
Heredity
Human Physiology & Anatomy
Microbiology
Physics

Physiology of Activity
Precalculus Mathematics
Rehabilitation Technology
Statistics
Technical Writing
Vertebrate Zoology

Often a bachelor degree is needed to apply for the competitive acceptance into professional (graduate) school.

OPTIONS WITHIN MAJOR

Prephysical Therapy

RECOMMENDED HIGH SCHOOL COURSES

Biology
Chemistry
English (3 Years)
History

Math (2 years)
Physiology
Social Problems

CAREERS	D.O.T. NUMBER	OUTLOOK	AVERAGE INITIAL SALARY
Graduate Degrees			
Physical Therapist	076.121-014	Excellent	$25,000
Professor	090.227-010	Good	27,000
Researcher		Good	28,000

PHYSICS AND ASTRONOMY

Physics inquires into the nature of the physical world and the laws governing our universe and is thus, basic to the physical sciences, engineering, technology, and the life sciences. Physicists observe various forms of energy and matter and their relationships in research that investigates the behavior of forces at work within the universe. The career objectives in Physics are broad, including scientific research, teaching, engineering, business, law, health, and related fields. Demand for well-trained physicists should increase, especially in applied areas, but many graduates (especially in astronomy) find they must go on to advanced training to prepare for job opportunities.

COURSE REQUIREMENTS

Acoustics
Analytical Geometry & Calculus
Astrophysics
Classical Field Theory
Descriptive Astronomy
Electricity and Magnetism
Environmental Physics
Experimental Physics
Mechanics
Nuclear Theory

Optics & Electromagnetic Theory
Ordinary Differential Equations
Physics
Plasma Physics
Quantum Theory
Quantum Mechanics
Space & Planetary Physics
Theoretical Physics
Thermal Physics

OPTIONS WITHIN MAJOR

Applied Physics
Astronomy

Education
Theoretical Physics

RECOMMENDED HIGH SCHOOL COURSES

Algebra (2 years)
Chemistry
Foreign Language

Geometry
Physics
Trigonometry

179

CAREERS	D.O.T. NUMBER	OUTLOOK	AVERAGE INITIAL SALARY
Bachelor Degrees			
Electro-optical Engineer	023.061-010	Good	$24,000
Environmentalist	029.081-010	Good	20,000
Health Physicist	079.021-010	Good	20,000
Meteorologist	012.067-014	Good/Fair	18,000
Solid-State Physicist		Good/Exc.	25,000
Teacher	091.227-010	Good	18,000
Graduate Degrees			
Astronomer	021.067-010	Fair/Good	27,000
Astrophysicist		Good	26,000
Biophysicist	041.061-034	Good	30,000
Chemical Physicist		Good	26,000
Electronic Physicist	023.061-010	Good/Exc.	31,000
Geophysicist	024.061-030	Good	24,000
Physicist	023.061-014	Good/Exc.	27,000
Plasma Physicist		Good	29,000
Professor	090.227-010	Fair	29,000
Theoretical Physicist	023.067-010	Excellent	30,000
Writer, Researcher		Good/Exc.	23,000

POLITICAL SCIENCE

Political Scientists study political behavior and institutions. Although some specialize in political theory or philosophy, most political scientists, particularly those specializing in public administration, concern themselves with the organization and operation of government at all levels in the United States and abroad. They explore such phenomena as public opinion, political parties, elections and special interest groups. They also focus on the workings of the bureaucracy, the presidency, congress, and the judicial system. Processes and techniques of public administration and public policymaking also are concerns of political scientists.

Approximately eighty percent of political scientists work in colleges or universities. Others work for government agencies, consulting firms, political organizations, research institutes, public interest groups, or business firms.

COURSE REQUIREMENTS

Comparative Politics
Comparative Studies
Constitutional Law
Foreign Area Studies
Foreign Policy
Government and Politics
International Law
International Politics

Public Administration & Policy
Political Behavior
Political Theory
Public Policy
State and Local Government
Urban Affairs
U. S. Politics

OPTIONS WITHIN MAJOR

Justice Administration
Political Science

Public Policy

RECOMMENDED HIGH SCHOOL COURSES

American Government
English (4 years)

History
Political Science

CAREERS	D.O.T. NUMBER	OUTLOOK	AVERAGE INITIAL SALARY
Bachelor Degrees			
Administration Trainee		Poor	$14,000
Columnist	131.067-010	Fair	19,000
Correspondent	131.267-018	Fair	24,000
Law Enforcement Trainee		Fair	15,000
Graduate Degrees			
Foreign Service	051.067-010	Good	29,000
Professor	090.227-010	Good	27,000
Research		Fair	26,000

PORTUGUESE

Like many language studies, Portuguese offers the graduate a variety of vocational opportunities as well as an understanding and appreciation for another language, culture, and people. Many graduate schools and professional studies (law, dentistry, medicine) require a second language, and many students consider language studies good training or further education. International law and business are also open to graduates as well as teaching on the secondary and college level. Owing to the limited number of teaching positions (especially on the high school level) many graduates are prepared for alternatives.

COURSE REQUIREMENTS

Composition
Conversation
Cultural Civilization
Grammar

Literature
Phonetics
Portuguese
Translation

OPTIONS WITHIN MAJOR

Business
Education

Interpretation/Translation

RECOMMENDED HIGH SCHOOL COURSES

Foreign Language
Geography
History

Humanities
Literature
Social Science

CAREERS	D.O.T. NUMBER	OUTLOOK	AVERAGE INITIAL SALARY
Bachelor Degrees			
Customs Official	168.267-022	Fair	$16,000
Foreign Service Officer	188.117-106	Fair	22,000
Import/Export Agent	184.117-022	Good	22,000
Intelligence Expert	059.267-010	Good	24,000
Interpreter	137.267-010	Fair/Good	19,000
Language Researcher	059.067-014	Fair	22,000
Public Relations Specialist	165.067-010	Fair/Good	25,000
Scientific Writer		Fair	24,000
Teacher	019.227-010	Poor	18,000
Translator	137.267-018	Good	19,000
Travel Agent	225.157-010	Good	12,000
Graduate Degrees			
Professor	090.227-010	Good	25,000
Scientific Linguist	059.067-014	Fair	24,000

PSYCHOLOGY

Psychology is the science that deals with the study of human behavior in a clinical, social, physiological, humanistic, and experimental way. Careers are available in secondary teaching, school counseling, clinical services, and industry. Advanced degrees are usually required for most opportunities, but high school teaching, probation work, psychometry, and various social services are open to those with a bachelor degrees. Graduate students in education, law, medicine, business, public administration, and social work find psychology a valuable undergraduate major.

COURSE REQUIREMENTS

Abnormal Psychology
Adolescent Psychology
Adult Psychology
Child Psychology
Clinical Psychology
Cognitive Processes
Developmental Psychology
Environmental Psychology
Exceptional Children
Leadership
Learning
Mental Disorders

Motivation
Organizational Psychology
Personality
Personnel Psychology
Psychobiology
Psychological Statistice
Psychological Testing
Research and Design
Sensation and Perception
Social Adjustment
Social Psychology

OPTIONS WITHIN MAJOR

Clinical Psychology
Counseling Psychology

Industrial Psychology
Social Psychology

RECOMMENDED HIGH SCHOOL COURSES

Algebra
English
Math

Psychology
Social Science

CAREERS	D.O.T. NUMBER	OUTLOOK	AVERAGE INITIAL SALARY
Bachelor Degrees			
Community Organization Officer	195.167-010	Fair	$16,000
Employment Counselor	045.107-010	Fair	20,000
Manual Arts Therapist	073.124-010	Fair	20,000
Probation/Parole Officer	195.167-030	Good	19,000
Recreational Therapist	076.124-014	Fair	19,000
Teacher	091.227-010	Good	18,000
Graduate Degrees			
Clinical Psychologist	045.107-022	Good/Exc.	30,000
Counseling Psychologist	045.107-026	Good	30,000
Educational Psychologist	045.067-010	Good	26,000
Engineering Psychologist	045.061-014	Fair	29,000
Experimental Psychologist	045.061-018	Good	26,000
Industrial Psychologist	045.107-030	Good	29,000
Industrial Psychometrist	045.067-018	Good	30,000
Industrial Therapist	076.167-010	Fair	30,000
Probation Officer	195.167-030	Good	23,000
Professor	090.227-010	Good	27,000
School Psychologist	045.107-034	Good	26,000
Social Psychologist	045.067-014	Good	23,000
Sports Psychologist		Good	28,000

PUBLIC RELATIONS

This professional program is designed to prepare qualified students for rewarding careers in public management and administration. The acquisition of attributes leading to positions of leadership of city, regional, state, and federal agencies is stressed. Many programs have internships that are required allowing the students to receive structured practical training.

COURSE REQUIREMENTS

Auditing and Evaluation
Budgeting
Business Ethics
Business Government Relations
City Planning and Development
Collective Bargaining
Cost Analysis
Debt Management
Equal Employment Opportunity
Financing Public Services
Investment Funds
Labor Relations
Managerial Economics
Manpower Planning
Organizational Development

Oral Communication
Personnel Management
Public Administration
Public Policy Analysis
Public Works
Quantitative Analysis
Sanitation
Systems Analysis
Tax Policy
Transportation
Urban and Regional Planning
Urban Management
Water Systems
Written Communication

OPTIONS WITHIN MAJOR

Finance
Government Administration
Personnel

Planning
Public Works

RECOMMENDED HIGH SCHOOL COURSES

Algebra
English

History

CAREERS	D.O.T. NUMBER	OUTLOOK	AVERAGE INITIAL SALARY
Bachelor Degrees			
Budget/Management Analyst	160.207-010	Good/Exc.	$20,000
Buyer	162.157-018	Fair/Good	22,000
Personnel Manager	166.117-018	Good	30,000
Purchasing Agent	162.157-038	Good	24,000
Safety Manager	012.167-014	Fair	23,000
Systems Analyst	012.167-066	Fair	25,000
Graduate Degrees			
Airport Manager	184.117-026	Fair	30,000
Director of Public Services	184.117-010	Fair	24,000
Director of Transportation	184.117-010	Fair	24,000
Professor	090.227-010	Good	27,000

PUBLIC RELATIONS

Public Relations workers help businesses, government, universities, and other organizations build and maintain a positive public image. Public Relations workers put together information that keeps the public aware of their employer's policies, activities, and accomplishments, and keeps management aware of public attitudes.

Manufacturing firms, public utilities and transportation companies, insurance companies, and trade and professional associations employ many public relations workers.

A sizable number work for government agencies, religious organizations, schools, colleges and universities, museums, health fields, and other human service organizations.

COURSE REQUIREMENTS

Advertising
Broadcasting
Business Administration
Creative Writing
Communications
Illustrative Photography
Journalism
Mass Communications
Media Design
Media Planning

Media Sales
Organizational Communication
Political Science
Public Relations Management
Public Relations Theory and
 Techniques
Psychology
Speech Composition
Writing & Production

OPTIONS WITHIN MAJOR

Business Administration
Education

Private Consulting

RECOMMENDED HIGH SCHOOL COURSES

Business Courses
English (4 years)
Journalism

Political Science
Psychology
Public Speaking

CAREERS	D.O.T. NUMBER	OUTLOOK	AVERAGE INITIAL SALARY
Bachelor Degrees			
Fundraiser	165.117-010	Fair	$21,000
Lobbyist	165.017-010	Fair	34,000
Promotion	165.167-010	Good	22,000
Public Relations Staff	165.067-010	Good/Exc.	19,000
Graduate Degrees			
Administrator		Good/Exc.	33,000
Consultant	189.167-010	Good	31,000
Managerial	189.167-022	Good/Exc.	26,000
Professor	090.227-010	Excellent	26,000
University Relations		Fair	31,000

RANGE MANAGEMENT

Range Management is sometimes called range science, range ecology, or range conservation. Professionals manage, improve, and protect range resources to maximize their use without damaging the environment. Employment opportunities are available in the federal government, principally in the Forest Service and the Soil Conservation Service of the Department of Agriculture, and the Bureau of Indian Affairs and the Bureau of Land departments, state land agencies, extension services, private industries, consulting firms, and large ranches.

COURSE REQUIREMENTS

Animal Nutrition
Biology
Chemistry
Computer Science
Conservation
Economics
Forestry
Hydrology
Inventory and Analysis
Law Enforcement

Livestock Management
Mathematics
Plant Ecology
Range Ecology
Range Plants
Resource Management
Physics
Soil Science
Watershed Management
Wildlife Management

OPTIONS WITHIN MAJOR

Agribusiness
Range Resources

Wildlife Resources

RECOMMENDED HIGH SCHOOL COURSES

Agriculture
Biology
Chemistry

English (3 years)
Math (2 years)
Speech

CAREERS	D.O.T. NUMBER	OUTLOOK	AVERAGE INITIAL SALARY
Bachelor Degrees			
Agricultural Appraiser	188.167-010	Good/Exc.	$21,000
Farm Manager		Fair	20,000
Range Manager	040.061-046	Good./Exc.	16,000
Vocational Agricultural Teacher	091.227-010	Fair	18,000
Graduate Degrees			
Professor	090.227-010	Good	26,000
Research		Good/Exc.	26,000

RECREATION MANAGEMENT

A career in recreation is a flexible opportunity of service to people in community centers, commercial organizations, hospitals, and the military. Increased leisure time and rising levels of per capita income for Americans will continue the demand for recreational activities throughout the nation. Graduates who enjoy indoor and outdoor activities, working with a variety of people, and planning and organizing will find adequate employment opportunities in recreational programs.

COURSE REQUIREMENTS

Aging and Leisure
Camp Aquatics
Crafts for Recreation
Community Recreation
Community Relations
Executive Dynamics
Facility Planning
Family Recreation
Land Survival
Leadership

Leisure in Contemporary Society
Mountaineering
Outdoor Recreation
Program Management
Public Facility Management
Skills Training
Social Recreation Leadership
Therapeutic Recreation
Youth Leadership

OPTIONS WITHIN MAJOR

Outdoor Recreation
Scouting

Youth Leadership

RECOMMENDED HIGH SCHOOL COURSES

Business
Crafts
Drama
Music

Psychology
Sociology
Speech

CAREERS	D.O.T. NUMBER	OUTLOOK	AVERAGE INITIAL SALARY
Bachelor Degrees			
Boy Scout Professional	153.117-018	Fair	$18,000
Hotel Recreation Manager	187.167-122	Good	16,000
Industrial Recreation Director		Fair	18,000
Municipal Recreation Administrator	187.137-010	Fair	27,000
Neighborhood Park Director	341.346-010	Good	15,000
Outdoor Recreation Director		Fair	15,000
Recreation Supervisor	195.167-026	Poor/Fair	16,000
Recreational Therapist	076.124-014	Fair	18,000
Graduate Degree			
Professor	090.227-010	Fair/Good	25,000

RUSSIAN

Increased interaction with the Soviet Union in science, industry, and government has escalated the need for trained graduates skilled in the Russian language. Apart from these practical language applications, a tremendous cultural wealth is contained in Russian literature and history. Currently, graduates are finding employment through teaching, government services, business, library work, and language-related research, although many find Russian useful in preparation for graduate school or professional studies.

COURSE REQUIREMENTS

Composition
Conversation
Cultural Civilization
Grammar

Literature
Phonetics
Russian
Translation

OPTIONS WITHIN MAJOR

Business
Education

Translation/Interpretation

RECOMMENDED HIGH SCHOOL COURSES

Foreign Language
Geography
History

Humanities
Literature
Social Science

CAREERS	D.O.T. NUMBER	OUTLOOK	AVERAGE INITIAL SALARY
Bachelor Degrees			
Customs Official	168.267-022	Fair	$16,000
Foreign Service Officer	188.117-106	Fair	22,000
Import/Export Agent	184.117-022	Good	22,000
Intelligence Expert	059.267-010	Good	24,000
Interpreter	137.267-010	Fair/Good	19,000
Language Researcher	059.067-014	Fair	22,000
Public Relations Specialist	165.067-010	Fair/Good	25,000
Scientific Writer		Fair	24,000
Teacher	019.227-010	Poor	18,000
Translator	137.267-018	Good	19,000
Travel Agent	225.157-010	Good	12,000
Graduate Degrees			
Professor	090.227-010	Good	25,000
Scientific Linguist	059.067-014	Fair	24,000

SECONDARY EDUCATION

Education in the public schools is a most important concern for over 15 million students and their parents and supplies jobs for over the one million teachers. All fifty states require certification in a teaching major and minor. Approved academic majors and minors are those subjects taught in the public schools. Openings are very competitive in the subjects that are not as widely taught or those areas with a surplus of qualified teachers. Vocational and Special Education are two areas of growing concern and opportunity. Teaching careers in music, foreign languages, art, physical education, and social studies find competition much keener.

COURSE REQUIREMENTS

Contemporary Issues
Educational Law
Educational Philosophy
Foundations in Reading
Individualized Instruction
Research Design
Secondary Curriculum

Theory of Teaching
Secondary Teacher Education
Social Foundations
Specific Courses in Teaching Major
Student Teaching
Teacher Aide Field Study
Teaching Fundamentals

OPTIONS WITHIN MAJOR

Art
Chemistry
Computers
Economics
English
English as a Second Language
French
German
Geography
Geology
Health
History
Home Economics

Industrial Arts
Journalism
Latin
Math
Music
Physical Education
Physics
Political Science
Psychology
Spanish
Speech
Sociology
Theatre Arts

RECOMMENDED HIGH SCHOOL COURSES

English (4 years)   Math (2 years)
History   Science

CAREERS	D.O.T. NUMBER	OUTLOOK	AVERAGE INITIAL SALARY
Bachelor Degrees			
Learning Specialist		Fair/Good	$18,000
Remedial Teacher		Good	18,000
Teacher	091.227-010	Fair/Good	18,000
Graduate Degrees			
Educational Administrator	009.117-026	Fair/Good	41,000
Principal	099.117-018	Fair	41,000
Professor	090.227-010	Fair	28,000

SOCIAL WORK

Social work in the health field involves programs and services that meet the special needs of the ill, disabled, elderly, or otherwise handicapped. Social workers deal with the emotional, social, cultural, and physical needs of patients in whom the effects of illness go far beyond bodily discomfort.

Sixty percent of all social workers provide direct services for public and voluntary agencies, including state departments of public assistance and community welfare and religious organizations. Most of the remainder are involved in social policy and planning, community organization, and administration in governmental agencies, primarily on the state and local level. Still others work for schools, hospitals, clinics, and other health facilities. A small but growing number of social workers are employed in business and industry.

COURSE REQUIREMENTS

Casework
Child Services
Child Welfare Services
Families at Risk
Family Health Care
Group Work
Human Behavior
Leadership and Group Action
Personality and Society
Psychology

Public Welfare
Social Legislation
Social Psychology
Social Services
Social Services for the Aging
Systems Theory
Social Welfare Policy
Social Work
Social Work Processes
Therapeutic Communications

OPTIONS WITHIN MAJOR

Community Mental Health
Counseling

Judicial Systems
Welfare Systems

RECOMMENDED HIGH SCHOOL COURSES

Biology
English
Psychology

Public Speaking
Sociology

CAREERS	D.O.T. NUMBER	OUTLOOK	AVERAGE INITIAL SALARY
Associate Degree			
Social Service Assistant		Good	$13,000
Bachelor Degrees			
Community Organization Worker	195.167-010	Fair	18,000
Delinquency Caseworker	195.107-026	Fair	17,000
Drug Control Officer	195.167-023	Fair	18,000
Parole Officer	195.167-030	Fair/Good	24,000
Probation Officer	195.167-034	Fair/Good	23,000
Social Caseworker	195.107-010	Fair	18,000
Social Groupworker	195.107-022	Fair	18,000
Welfare Officer	195.117-010	Poor	18,000
Graduate Degrees			
Certified Social Worker (ASCW)		Good	24,000
Graduate Social Worker (MSW)		Good/Exc.	25,000
Medical Social Worker	195.107-030	Fair	23,000
Professor	090.227-010	Good	28,000
Psychiatric Social Worker	195.107-038	Fair/Good	28,000
School Social Worker	195.107-038	Fair/Good	22,000
Social Worker	195.107-010	Good	21,000
Social Worker Fellow (DSW)		Good	30,000

SOCIOLOGY

Sociology is the study of human group behavior and interaction within families, communities, formal organizations, and societies. Sociologists study the social institutions formed by mankind and the influence which these institutions have upon the individual. Most sociologists are employed by universities and colleges, teaching and conducting research, but there are also opportunities in industry, organizations, and some secondary schools.

COURSE REQUIREMENTS

Applied Sociology
Collective Behavior
Deviance and Social Control
Juvenile Delinquency
Medical Sociology
Mental Health Services
Methods of Research in Sociology
Sport Sociology
Social Change

Social Organization
Social Problems
Social Psychology
Social Statistics
Social Stratification
Sociological Analysis
Sociology
Sociology of the Family
World Populations

OPTIONS WITHIN MAJOR

Applied Sociology
General Sociology

Professional Sociology
Secondary Education

RECOMMENDED HIGH SCHOOL COURSES

English (4 years)
History
Mathematics

Psychology
Sociology

CAREERS	D.O.T. NUMBER	OUTLOOK	AVERAGE INITIAL SALARY
Bachelor Degrees			
Administrative Assistant	169.167-010	Fair/Good	$15,000
Sales Representative	261.257-030	Fair	16,000
Community Organization Worker	195.167-010	Fair	19,000
Delinquency Caseworker	195.107-026	Fair	18,000
Social Case Worker	195.107-010	Fair	18,000
Teacher	091.227-010	Fair	18,000
Graduate Degrees			
Criminologist	054.067-010	Fair/Good	22,000
Industrial Sociologist	054.067-010	Good	23,000
Penologist	054.067-014	Fair	24,000
Professor/Researcher	090.227-010	Good	27,000
Rural Sociologist	054.067-014	Fair	22,000
Social Ecologist	054.067-010	Fair	24,000
Social Pathologist		Fair/Good	25,000
Urban Sociologist	054.067-010	Good	25,000

SPANISH

Spanish is one of the major languages in the world, ranking fifth in the number of native speakers (second only to English in the Western Hemisphere). In high schools, Spanish is the most frequently studied foreign language, accounting for almost 40 percent of all foreign language students. Besides teaching, bilingual graduates are needed in all phases of life to serve the millions of Spanish-speaking Americans in the Southwest and other areas.

COURSE REQUIREMENTS

Conversation
Composition
Cultural Civilization
Grammar

Literature
Phonetics
Spanish
Translation

OPTIONS WITHIN MAJOR

Business
Education

Translation/ Interpretation

RECOMMENDED HIGH SCHOOL COURSES

Geography
History
Humanities

Literature
Spanish
Social Science

CAREERS	D.O.T. NUMBER	OUTLOOK	AVERAGE INITIAL SALARY
Bachelor Degrees			
Customs Official	168.267-022	Fair	$16,000
Foreign Service Officer	188.117-106	Fair	22,000
Import/Export Agent	184.117-022	Good	22,000
Intelligence Expert	059.267-010	Good	24,000
Interpreter	137.267-010	Fair/Good	19,000
Language Researcher	059.067-014	Fair	22,000
Public Relations Specialist	165.067-010	Fair/Good	25,000
Scientific Writer		Fair	24,000
Teacher	091.227-010	Poor	18,000
Translator	137.267-018	Good	19,000
Travel Agent	225.157-010	Good	12,000
Graduate Degrees			
Professor	090.227-010	Good	25,000
Scientific Linguist	059.067-014	Fair	24,000

SPECIAL EDUCATION

An increasing awareness of children with handicaps has influenced the development of programs that offer specific training for teachers. Special education programs in the public schools are designed to help students who are severely intellectually handicapped, severely learning disabled, severely emotionally handicapped, and the mildly learning handicapped to study in resource room environments. The special education program may be offered as an individual program, or combined with a major in elementary education.

COURSE REQUIREMENTS

Assessing Learning Dysfunctions
Behavior Development
Computers in Education
Educational Psychology
Exceptional Children in School
Human Development
Learning Disabilities
Learning Theory

Psychology
Resource Teaching
Severely Emotionally Disabled
Severely Intellectually Disabled
Severely Learning Disabled
Teaching Math
Teaching Reading
Teaching Science

OPTIONS WITHIN MAJOR

Emotionally Disabled
Intellectually Disabled

Learning Disabled
Resource Teaching

RECOMMENDED HIGH SCHOOL COURSES

English
Math

Natural Sciences
Social Sciences

CAREERS	D.O.T. NUMBER	OUTLOOK	AVERAGE INITIAL SALARY
Bachelor Degrees			
Teacher of the Handicapped	094.227-018	Excellent	$18,000
Teacher of the Mentally Retarded	094.227-022	Excellent	18,000
Graduate Degrees			
Administrator	099.117-026	Fair/Good	38,000
Professor	099.227-010	Excellent	28,000

SPEECH PATHOLOGY
AND AUDIOLOGY

Speech pathologists and audiologists provide direct services for people who have speech or hearing impairment. The speech pathologist works with children and adults who have speech, language, and voice disorders. The audiologist primarily assesses and treats hearing problems.

Nearly one-half of speech pathologists and audiologists work in public schools. Colleges and universities employ many in classrooms, clinics, and research centers. The rest work in hospitals, speech and hearing centers, government agencies, industry, and private practice.

COURSE REQUIREMENTS

Acoustics
Analysis of Speech Production
Audiology
Auditory Processes
Aural Rehabilitation
Biology
Child Psychology
Communicative Disorders
Disorders of Articulation
Language Abilities

Linguistics
Phonetics
Psychological Aspects of
Communication
Semantics
Sociology
Speech Anatomy
Speech Physiology
Remediation Communication
Disorders

OPTIONS WITHIN MAJOR

Clinical
Education

Research

RECOMMENDED HIGH SCHOOL COURSES

Anatomy
Biology
English (4 years)
Math (3 years)

Physiology
Psychology
Public Speaking

CAREERS	D.O.T. NUMBER	OUTLOOK	AVERAGE INITIAL SALARY
Graduate Degrees			
Audiologist	076.101-010	Good/Exc.	$23,000
Speech Pathologist	076.107-010	Good/Exc.	29,000
Professor	090.227-010	Good/Exc.	28,000

STATISTICS

The statistician is an applied mathematician who uses design and analysis, operations research, probability theory, and other statistical tools to make decisions and solve problems for social scientists, biologists, economists, businessmen, and others who conduct research and collect data. Federal and state agencies, large industrial firms, and pharmaceutical companies are major employers of statisticians in discovering possible election outcomes, optimal methods and products, optimal business location, and a variety of sampling schemes. Graduates also play a key role in the field of actuarial science.

COURSE REQUIREMENTS

Analytical Geometry/Calculus
Categorical Data
Data Analysis
Experimental Design
Mathematical Statistics
Nonparametric Methods
Operation Research
Probability

Quality Control
Regression Analysis
Statistical Methods
Statistics
Survey Sampling
Theory of Linear Models
Theory of Statistics

OPTIONS WITHIN MAJOR

Actuarial Sciences
Computer Service

Research
Statistics

RECOMMENDED HIGH SCHOOL COURSES

Biology
Chemistry
Computer Science

English (4 years)
Math (3 years)
Physics

CAREERS	D.O.T. NUMBER	OUTLOOK	AVERAGE INITIAL SALARY
Bachelor Degrees			
Actuary	020.167-010	Good/Exc.	$27,000
Computer Programmer	007.167-018	Excellent	23,000
Market/Operating Research Analyst	050.067-014	Good/Exc.	24,000
Quality Controller	012.167-054	Excellent	23,000
Systems Analyst	012.167-060	Excellent	26,000
Graduate Degrees			
Professor	090.227-010	Excellent	28,000
Research		Excellent	31,000
Systems Analyst	012.167-060	Excellent	33,000

THEATRE AND CINEMATIC ARTS

Theatre and cinematic arts attempt to provide the public with entertainment to fulfill their aesthetic needs. Graduates receive training in costuming, set design, acting, directing, play writing, musical theatre, motion picture and TV production, children's drama, or theatre arts education. Many positions in the drama and film industries are highly competitive and openings in education vary from area to area. Employment opportunities and starting salaries are based on training, experience, and ability.

COURSE REQUIREMENTS

Acting
Acting for Cinema/Stage
Art of Interpretation
Audiovisual Production
Child Drama
Cinematography
Costume Design
Criticism of Film Art
Dialects
Directing
Directing the One-Act Play
Directing Theory
Film Editing
Film Sound

Motion Picture Art
Musical
Musical Theatre
Playwriting
Puppetry
Stage Makeup
Storytelling
Theater for Children
Theater History
Theater Management
Theatrical Design
Technical Theatre
Voice, Diction, & Interpretation

OPTIONS WITHIN MAJOR

Acting
Child Drama
Costume Design
Designer/Technician
Directing

Directing
Motion Picture and TV Production
Playwriting
Theatre Arts Education

RECOMMENDED HIGH SCHOOL COURSES

English (4 years)   Literature
Drama   Speech
Forensics

CAREERS	D.O.T. NUMBER	OUTLOOK	AVERAGE INITIAL SALARY
Associate Degrees			
Costume Specialist	346.374-010	Good	$18,000
Performance Specialist		Fair	17,000
Bachelor Degrees			
Actor	150.047-010	Fair	Varies
Drama Coach	150.027-010	Fair	21,000
Director	150.067-010	Fair/Good	29,000
Motion Picture/TV Director	159.167-010	Fair	29,000
Playwright	131.067-038	Fair/Good	Varies
Teacher	150.027-014	Good	18,000
Technical Director		Good	27,000
Graduate Degree			
Professor	090.227-010	Fair	28,000

VETERINARY MEDICINE

The majority of veterinarians are general practitioners who diagnose, treat, and control disease and injury in animals. Practice ranges from veterinary hospitals and clinics to farms and ranches. Specialists in veterinary medicine generally treat pets and small animals, although some deal with cattle, poultry, horse, or sheep care. Many veterinarians perform research related to animal disease and also serve as inspectors for local and federal government agencies. Although the need for many more veterinarians exists, there are only 18 veterinary schools and competition for admission is keen.

COURSE REQUIREMENTS

Most students accepted to Veterinary School have a bachelor degree. Courses include the following:

Animal Parasitology
Animal Production
Biochemistry
Biology
Calculus
College Algebra
College Chemistry
Feeds and Feeding

Fundamentals of Animal Breeding
Genetics
Invertebrate Zoology
Microbiology
Organic Chemistry
Pathology
Physics
Virology

Professional school courses are a continuation of those above in more depth and with clinical experiences.

OPTIONS WITHIN MAJOR

Anatomy
Bacteriology
Laboratory Animal Care
Parasitology
Pathology

Pharmacology
Physiology
Radiology
Virology

213

RECOMMENDED HIGH SCHOOL COURSES

Biology
Chemistry
English (4 years)

Math (3 years)
Physics
Physiology

CAREERS	D.O.T. NUMBER	OUTLOOK	AVERAGE INITIAL SALARY
Graduate Degrees			
Veterinarian	073.101-010	Excellent	$35,000
Veterinary Anatomist	073.061-014	Excellent	36,000
Veterinary Bacteriologist	073.061-018	Good	31,000
Veterinary Epidemologist	073.061-022	Excellent	32,000
Veterinary Pathologist	073.061-030	Excellent	40,000
Veterinary Physiologist	073.061-038	Excellent	38,000
Veterinary Virologist	073.061-042	Excellent	37,000

WILDLIFE MANAGEMENT

Wildlife Specialists are professionals concerned with protecting and controlling our natural resources of soil, water, plants, and animals for the purpose of maintaining desired numbers of animals in accordance with public interest and welfare.

Employment opportunities are found with the state and federal agencies, Peace Corps, forest industry, state forestry agencies, cities, counties, educational institutions, consultants and others. Also, private laboratories and numerous scientifically-based foundations have wildlife specialists on their staffs. Some wildlife specialists operate shooting or hunting reserves, manage private clubs, or act as writers or photographers of outdoor subjects.

COURSE REQUIREMENTS

Algebra
Biology
Botany
Calculus
Chemistry
Ecology
Economics
Environmental Conservation
Fish and Wildlife Biology

Fishery & Biology Management
Mammalogy
Plant Classification
Physics
Public Relations
Public Speaking
Statistics
Soil Science

OPTIONS WITHIN MAJOR

Wildlife Administration

Wildlife Biology

RECOMMENDED HIGH SCHOOL COURSES

Biology
Chemistry
English (3 years)
History

Mathematics (3 years)
Physics
Social Studies

CAREERS	D.O.T. NUMBER	OUTLOOK	AVERAGE INITIAL SALARY
Associate Degree			
Forestry Technician	040.061-062	Fair/Good	$15,000
Bachelor Degrees			
Administrator	180.167-038	Poor	25,000
Conservation Officer	379.167-010	Poor	15,000
Photographer	143.457-010	Poor	21,000
Wildlife Biologist	041.061-030	Poor/Fair	20,000
Wildlife Manager	379.137-018	Poor/Fair	22,000
Graduate Degree			
Professor		Fair	26,000

YOUTH LEADERSHIP

As the strength of the American home diminishes, the need for qualified leaders to work with youth increases. Youth leadership prepares such leaders to work in agencies such as the Boy Scouts of America, YMCA, YWCA, Boys Club of America, Camp Fire Girls, Girl Scouts, 4-H, Junior achievements, and any other organization that serves the youth. The outdoor education program in survival and other pioneering programs require skilled development and direction as they seek to positively change behavior. Aside from professional training, students are prepared to assist community and church volunteer programs.

COURSE REQUIREMENTS

Camp Administration
Camp Counseling
Career Internship
Career Observations
Community Relationships
Executive Dynamics
Executive Field Training Seminar
Finance

First-aid/Emergency Care
Intramural Sports
Introduction to Youth Leadership
Keys to Leadership
Moving Camps
Outdoor Leadership
Practicum
Trail Leadership

OPTIONS WITHIN MAJOR

Agency Emphasis

Outdoor Education Emphasis

RECOMMENDED HIGH SCHOOL COURSES

Biological Sciences
Communications
English (3 years

Extra-Curricular Activities
Speech

CAREERS	D.O.T. NUMBER	OUTLOOK	AVERAGE INITIAL SALARY
Bachelor Degrees			
Boy Scout Professional	153.117-018	Fair	$18,000
Business Manager	189.167-022	Good	16,000
County Extension Agent	096.127-014	Fair	25,000
Field Staff Executive	189.267-010	Fair/Good	18,000
Training Director	166.227-010	Good	17,000
Youth Agency Admin.	096.127-022	Good/Exc.	20,000

ZOOLOGY

Zoologists deal with all aspects of animal life (including man) on submicroscopic, microscopic, and macroscopic levels. Zoologists must become familiar with knowledge and techniques of chemistry, physics. math and several types of laboratories. With this broad background, zoologists serve as laboratory and X-ray technicians, dental hygienists, pharmaceutical lab specialists, as well as in government and private research, and business. Many preprofessional students of dentistry, medicine, and other health services major in zoology.

COURSE REQUIREMENTS

Animal Systemics	Ichthyology
Aquaculture	Insect Morphology
Bioethics	Insects
Cell & Developmental Biology	Invertebrate Zoology
Ecology	Mammalogy
Embryology	Marine Biology
Entomology	Medical Parasitology
Environmental Biology	Microbiology
Evolution Theory	Organic Chemistry
Genetics	Ornithology
Heredity and Reproduction	Physiology
Herpetology	Plant Science
Histology	Vertebrate Zoology
Human Anatomy	Zoology
Human Physiology	

OPTIONS WITHIN MAJOR

Applied Zoology	Preprofessional
Education	Research

RECOMMENDED HIGH SCHOOL COURSES

Biology	English
Chemistry	Math

CAREERS	D.O.T. NUMBER	OUTLOOK	AVERAGE INITIAL SALARY
Bachelor Degrees			
Biologist	041.061-030	Fair	$20,000
Park Naturalist	049.127-010	Fair/Good	18,000
Teacher	091.227-010	Good	18,000
Wildlife Biologist	041.061-030	Fair/Good	20,000
Wildlife Manager	379.137-018	Poor	22,000
Zoologist	041.061-090	Fair/Good	22,000
Graduate Degrees			
Animal Physiologist	041.061-078	Fair/Good	23,000
Aquatic Biologist	041.061-020	Fair	23,000
Biologist	041.061-030	Good	26,000
Biophysicist	041.061-034	Fair	29,000
Cytologist	041.061-042	Fair	25,000
Entomologist	041.061-046	Good	20,000
Geneticist	041.061-054	Excellent	21,000
Histopathologist	041.061-090	Excellent	25,000
Professor	090.227-010	Good	28,000

APPENDICES

Appendix A–Interpreting the *Dictionary of Occupational Titles*

This government publication is often found in the offices of most counselors or in career centers and libraries. It provides descriptions of over 12,000 jobs and is an important reference for you to know about.

If an occupation is included in this publication, it has a reference number which is actually a code. By looking up the title, you can read a brief description about the job and environment along with some ideas of tasks used on the job.

The sample number is broken down into a working code below:

SAMPLE

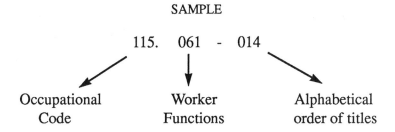

Occupational Code	Worker Functions	Alphabetical order of titles

Occupational Code

The first three digits classify specific occupational groups. The first digit represents 9 cluster occupations including:

0/1 Professional, Technical, and Managerial	5 Processing
2 Clerical and Sales	6 Machine Tools
3 Service	7 Bench Trades
4 Agricultural, Fishing, and Forestry	8 Structural Work
	9 Miscellaneous

Degrees associated with college majors are found mostly in the 0/1 and 2 occupational group. The second two digits of the occupational code are categorized into 82 specific divisions such as engineering, education, music, etc.

Worker Function

The second set of 3 digits identifies the types of tasks most often associated or used in the specific occupation. When working, according to this government publication, we perform specific tasks centered around DATA, PEOPLE, or THINGS. A particular occupation may emphasize each of these three categories with different intensities. The D.O.T. simply lists the major types of tasks associated with each of the 3 categories.

4th Digit = **Data**	5th Digit = **People**	6th Digit = **Things**
0 Synthesizing	0 Mentoring	0 Setting up
1 Coordinating	1 Negotiating	1 Precision Working
2 Analyzing	2 Instructing	2 Operating-Controling
3 Compiling	3 Supervising	3 Driving-Operating
4 Computing	4 Diverting	4 Manipulating
5 Copying	5 Persuading	5 Tending
6 Comparing	6 Speaking-signaling	6 Feeding
	7 Serving	7 Handling
	8 Taking Instructions	

Alphabetical Order of Titles

The last 3 digits are merely the general listing of occupations withing the first six digits.

EXAMPLE

Occupation: Civil Engineering

D.O.T. Number: 005-061-014

   0 Professional, Technical, and Management
  05 Engineering
   0 Synthesizing data
   6 Speaking/signaling with people
   1 Precision working with things
014 Alphabetical listing of Civil Engineering

Appendix B–Educational Alternatives

Specialized Technical School
Short-term, 6 to 24 month specialized training in a technical area characterizes this type of training. Very few "nonessential" classes are required. Quite often a technical school provides only one area of emphasis such as dental technology, cosmetology, business, etc.

Technical College
Here, general education courses are mixed with technical training. A technical college may offer associate degrees that transfer to a four-year college or university. More often, programs are specifically designed to prepare students for careers upon completion.

Two-Year Community College
These are also called junior colleges. While short-term degrees are offered, most students attend these schools in preparation for four-year colleges or universities. You can earn an associate degree in two years or transfer anytime after the first enrollment.

Four-Year College
An associate degree or bachelor degree can be earned at this level of higher education. Some four-year colleges also offer limited graduate degrees. A variety of courses are available.

University
A university provides a wide variety of coursework and several levels of degrees. A university is divided into several "colleges" such as the College of Business or the College of Biological Sciences. Each college is composed of several departments. A department may offer one or more majors. Degrees range from associate, bachelor, master, and doctoral programs.

Transfer of Credit
Students often accumulate credit at one school then transfer to another one in order to complete a degree. If courses are college level courses, the credit will transfer from one accredited institution to another. When a student transfers to a new school, official transcripts of all credits must be sent from all previous institutions to the admissions office of the new institution.

Graduation Requirements

Credit Hour
Credit is awarded for courses based on the amount of time spent in class per week. For example, a 5-credit course generally requires you to be in class 5 periods each week. A 2-hour class requires 2 class periods per week. Often a laboratory period is extra. An average load is 14 to 17 quarter or semester hours for each registration.

Semester Hour
There are three semesters in one year. One academic year equals two semesters. Approximately 130 semester hours are needed to graduate.

Transfer
When you transfer from a quarter system to a semester system, it may appear that you lose credits. Just remember that there are three quarters but only two semesters in each academic year. Therefore, three quarter hours credit equals two semester hours credit.

Graduation
This denotes an academic accomplishment that has been outlined by the school. Basic requirements usually include:

1. Completing general education courses
2. Completing courses in a major field of study
3. Completing a minimum number of credit hours
4. Passing specifically required examinations or courses

Degrees
Various degrees are awarded by schools. A complete listing is found on the following pages. The last four are usually obtained only at a four-year college or university.

Types of Degrees
1. **Certificate.** A six to twelve month course
2. **Junior College Degree.** A one-year course
3. **Associate Degree of Applied Science or Arts.** A two-year degree that usually does not transfer all credits to a college or university
4. **Associate of Arts or Science.** A two-year degree used for job preparation or transferring
5. **Bachelor of Arts or Science.** A four-year degree

6. **Master of Arts, or Science, Engineering, Business, etc.** A one-to-two year program beyond the bachelor level
7. **Doctor of Education, Philosophy, Medicine, etc.** A two-to-four year program beyond the master level

General Education

To ensure a student is well-educated, colleges and universities require a number of classes in a variety of areas. Breadth of knowledge is at least as important as depth of knowledge.

Major

When you decide on a speciality you want, then you select a major. Each major consists of at least one-third to one-half of the entire graduation requirements. The courses are usually sequential, starting with the simple and moving to the more technical and complex.

Ideas on Admissions

Getting admitted to a college of your choice takes time and effective planning. Often, what you have accomplished as early as the ninth grade will impact your chances for admissions. The closer you get to graduation, the more important it will become to know clearly the steps that will help. Your counselors are an indispensable part of your admissions efforts. They are in contact with college representatives and have both experience and information that will be helpful. Below is a sequence that can become meaningful to you. It is followed by a description of each step.

1. Take College Prep Courses
2. Work Hard in the Classes
3. Take the College Admissions Tests
4. Apply for Admissions
5. Select a College
6. Implement Your Plan

Take College Prep Courses

Beginning with the ninth grade, the specific high school courses that you choose will be important in your admissions to college. Most colleges, especially those universities that cannot accept all the applicants that apply, have outlined specific courses that are designated college prep. A rule of thumb is, that if a class is both required for graduation and is an academically oriented course, it is considered college prep. Examples would be U.S. history, algebra II, foreign languages, and laboratory sciences. Be careful, because such classes as journalism and psychology are often thought to be college prep by students, but not by admissions committees who evaluate high school transcripts.

Selective colleges and universities are requesting that from 50% to 70% of your classes in high school be college prep. Avoid the reasoning that you will build your grades by taking non-college prep courses. On the other hand, look for the opportunity to take honors and especially advanced placement courses. A student's seriousness about higher education is often reflected in the types of classes taken.

Work Hard in the Classes

Grades and grade point averages are calculated, for admissions decisions, from the ninth through the twelfth grades. Typically an "A" = 4 points, "B" = 3 points, "C" = 2 points, and "D" = 1 point. You can calculate your grade point average by (1) multiplying the units of each class times the points earned for the grade of the class—this is called the grade points, (2) add up the total units for all the classes, (3) add the grade points for all the classes, and (4) divide the total grade points, by the total number of units.

Most colleges look at the total or cumulative grade point average (GPA) for all your classes. However, there are some colleges and universities who are highly selective, who also want the GPA for college prep courses. Although not common, in these colleges with highly selective admissions, higher weighted points are given for honors and advanced placement courses (that is, an "A" might equal more than 4 points, etc.). You will need to check with the particular college for which you have interest to know their policies.

Take the College Admissions Tests

The two most frequently given college entrance tests are the Scholastic Aptitude Test (SAT) and the American College Test (ACT). Colleges usually have a preference for the test they want you to take. Both tests are given on specific dates at a specific place. Approximately six weeks is required between the time you apply for the test and the date you will take it. If you do not apply on time, the testing companies will not send a test for you.

The SAT has a verbal and a numerical section. The ACT tests in English, math, social science, and natural science. You will be compared against all other sudents who take the test in the nation, your state, and your school. When colleges receive the results of your tests, your score will be compared to students in that school.

A large controversy exists as to whether you can prepare for the tests. Studies have resulted in conflicting findings. It is, however, to your advantage to become familiar with the types of questions you will be encountering on the tests. Your counselor will be able to help you with booklets provided from the testing company.

Apply for Admissions

Before applying for admissions to a college, find out about their admissions policies. For example, there are three types of admissions. Colleges with an *open* admissions policy require a high school diploma or its equivalent and typically have a minimum age factor. Many colleges have a *selective* admissions policy, which requires specific information such as GPA and college entrance examination scores. These colleges have established minimum requirements that are necessary for a student to attain regarding grades and test results. A third category includes those colleges (typically large universities that have graduate programs and conduct research) who have a *highly selective* policy for admissions. They also require GPA and test scores, but often require other information such as percent of your high school courses that are college prep, GPA on your college prep courses, letters of recommendations, an essay from you to identify your educational goals and to test your writing ability, interviews, and a record of extra-curricular activities. If the college is sponsored by a church, an endorsement from your ecclesiastical leader may be requested.

When letters of recommendation are requested, understand that the college is interested in knowing how well you can do academically. Therefore, avoid the temptation of having a friend, community leader, or neighbor write a letter elaborating on other than educational endeavors. Those letters that have the most influence are from teachers of strong academic courses.

Students are sometimes disappointed when they fail to get their application completed and to the college before the deadline. Most colleges have deadlines, and those with selective or highly selective admissions policies hold stictly to that deadline.

Your counselor typically has copies of local institutions and those where many of the sudents in your school have traditionally enrolled. If they are not readily available, the counselor can help you find where to write for catalogs and application materials.

Select a College

When selecting a college there are several factors to consider. One of the first is finances. Limited finances may suggest that you attend a college while living at home. Costs of housing and food are often expensive. The cost of tuition also influences finances. Work with your counselor to identify all the costs that you will incur at colleges you are considering. Compare the costs to your financial resources.

Another important factor to consider is whether the college has the academic major that you want to study. If you have not chosen a major, this may not be a significant determinant. However, if you are considering a major such as nursing or engineering, it is important to begin at the college from which you want to graduate. The reason is that courses in these programs are highly sequential and begin the first semester that you enroll. If you miss the first sequence, you may have to wait a complete year for the sequence to begin again. Because the number of majors that are very structured is increasing, it is usually a good practice to start at the school from which you want to get your degree.

If you plan to attend a community college in order to take your general education courses, and transfer to a four-year college or university, select your courses carefully. While all college level courses transfer from one accredited insitution to another, they may not fit into the category you intended. For example, a class that is considered a general education course in physical science at a community college may not be classified as the same in a particular four-year college. It will transfer as an elective, but not in the area you intended. The same is also true for classes in one's major. Most community colleges have lists of their courses and how they transfer to specific local institutions. Acquire those lists and select your courses with your transfer in mind.

Other considerations are important in selecting a college. A few are distance from home, size of the student body, athletic or fine arts programs, and work opportunities. Take time and consider carefully your choice. College is costly in both time and money.

Implement Your Plan

The time between your application for admissions and when you go to school, is important. Here are a few things to consider.

When you apply for admissions, the application will usually ask for the major you intend to pursue. Even if you are not certain, select a major that you are considering and list it. Most colleges will send you valuable information about that particular major, which will include the courses they recommend for your first enrollment period.

Check on housing and make the necessary arrangements early to increase the probability of getting with a desired roommate or in an area of your liking. If a job is necessary for you, find out how to apply for on-campus jobs and locate off-campus possibilities; begin aggressively pursuing potential opportunities. Contact the financial aids office early and continue this association until you are satisfied that you have your financial aids package firmly in place.

Appendix C–Your Interest Areas

Different people like different things. Likes are based in part on the experiences you have had and how well you have enjoyed them. There may also be areas of interest which you know little about or with which you have had little experience.

As one explores educational majors and various occupations, it is important to look at the interests you have and compare them with various occupations or categories of occupations. As you make this comparison, many of your interest areas may require knowledge and skills that you currently do not have.

A government task force has developed 12 categories of interest: Artistic, Scientific, Plants and Animals, Protective, Mechanical, Industrial, Business Detail, Selling, Accommodating, Humanitarian, Leading-Influencing, and Physical Performing. In addition, the 12 interest areas are divided into Work Groups. A description of the Work Groups for each Interest Area is listed below. More information on each of the 12 Interest Areas and their Work Groups can be found in the *Guide for Occupational Exploration* developed by the U.S. Department of Labor and in *The Enhanced Guide for Occupational Exploration* (©1991). This book also provides descriptions for 2,500 jobs organized into these categories.

Read the explanations of the 35 Work Groups below. Put a checkmark in front of the Work Groups that interest you. Page numbers are listed for each work group that corresponds to majors in *The Career Connection*.

ARTISTIC: Expressing ideas or feelings creatively
__Literary Arts 49, 79, 109, 127, 171, 209
Working with written expression such as editing, creative writing, critiquing, or publishing
__Visual Arts 23, 47, 59, 61
Creating original art through studio work, commercial art instructing, and directing
__Performing Arts: Drama 209
Working in dramatic productions in the areas of performing, composing, arranging, instructing, and directing
__Performing Arts: Music 157
Participating in the musical arena by vocal performing, composing, arranging, instructing, and directing
__Performing Arts: Dance 55
Contributing to dance through performance, instruction, and choreography

SCIENTIFIC: Analyzing information gathered through research to solve problems in the natural world

__Physical Sciences 37, 99, 101, 143, 167, 177
Applying technology and research in the study of non-living things
__Life Sciences 27, 89, 91, 113, 153, 217
Understanding living things through animal specialization, plant specialization, and food research
__Medical Sciences 57, 63, 71, 105, 107, 149, 161, 170, 211, 217
Relieving human or animal distress by means of dentistry, veterinary medicine, health specialities, services, and surgery
__Laboratory Technology 147
Assisting physical scientists or life scientists by conducting and recording research for them

PLANTS AND ANIMALS: Studying plants and animals in their natural environment

__Managerial Work: Plants and Animals 17, 91, 113, 129, 189, 213
Managing businesses that deal with plants and animals such as farming, speciality breeding, speciality cropping, forestry, and logging

PROTECTIVE: Guarding the lives and property of others

__Safety and Law Enforcement 163
Compelling others to obey the laws through positions in management and investigation

MECHANICAL: Use of hands and tools to create or repair objects

__Engineering 7, 35, 41, 73, 75, 145, 151, 155
Generating and carrying out ideas for construction projects in research, environmental protection, systems design, sales engineering testing, quality control, design, general engineering, work planning and utilization
__Engineering Technology 21, 59, 61, 65, 75, 139
Gathering information for others as a surveyor, drafter, expediter and coordinator in the areas of petroleum, electrical-electronic industry, mechanics, environmental control, packaging, and storing
__Systems Operation 117
Servicing equipment that is part of a larger system as in electricity generation and transmission; stationary engineering; oil, gas, and water distribution; and processing

__Quality Control 117__

Checking products for compliance with set standards in the mechanical, electrical, environmental, petroleum, structural, logging, and lumber fields

INDUSTRIAL: Applying skills to perform repetitive, structured tasks

(A college degree is not necessary for most of the jobs in this area.)

BUSINESS DETAIL: Carrying out specified tasks in an office setting

__Administration Detail 29, 31, 49, 87, 105, 115, 121, 141, 185, 187__

Tending to the clerical work in an office through interviewing, administrative, secretarial work, financial work, certifying, investigation, and test administration

__Mathematical Detail 3__

Overseeing the mathematical details in an office through reporting and analysis, accounting, billing, rate computation, payroll, timekeeping, bookkeeping and book auditing

__Clerical Machine Operation 29, 121__

Use of machines such as computers and keyboard machines to organize data

__Clerical Handling 29, 121__

Carrying out tasks in a business which require little skill such as filing, sorting, distributing, and general clerical work

SELLING: Presenting goods or services to people and persuading them to purchase

__Sales Technology 31, 85, 123, 141, 187__

Selling technical products and services and consulting with customers as to purchasing and sales

__General Sales 31, 47, 59, 87, 141__

Demonstrating and selling products in many different settings such as wholesale, retail, real estate, and services

ACCOMMODATING: Caring for the needs of others

(A college degree is not necessary for most of the jobs in this area.)

HUMANITARIAN: Caring for the health needs of others

__Social Services 71, 165, 183, 197, 199, 215__

Meeting with groups or individuals to help them understand and deal with their problems from a religious or a counseling viewpoint

__Nursing, Therapy, and Specialized Teaching Services 71, 161, 165, 169, 175, 203, 205
Aiding in improving the physical and emotional health of others as a nurse, therapist, or teacher
__Child and Adult Care 67, 77, 161, 197
Helping others meet their physical needs through data collection, patient care, and general care such as foster care

LEADING-INFLUENCING: Use of leadership abilities and other skills to guide people in thought and action
__Mathematical and Statistics 53, 69, 207
Applying mathematics skills in data processing design and data analysis
__Education and Library Science 51, 77, 111, 119, 135, 195, 203
Working in an educational setting as a librarian or as a teacher of subjects such as home economics and vocational studies
__Social Research 5, 69, 71, 109, 137, 179, 183, 199
Conducting psychological, sociological, historical, occupational and economic research on individuals or groups
__Law 133
Attending to the legal matters of others through legal practice, document preparation, justice administration, and conciliation
__Business Administration 31, 87, 123, 141, 185
Making decisions and supervising others in government and nongovernment establishments
__Finance 85, 87, 141
Applying mathematical skills to handle the financial aspects of a business such as accounting, auditing, record keeping, brokering, and budgeting
__Service Administration 105, 163, 165, 173, 197, 199, 215
Overseeing social, health, safety, education and recreation programs provided by businesses which provide such services
__Communications 49, 79, 127, 187, 209
Working with the media such as editing, writing, broadcasting, translating and interpreting factual information
__Promotion 5, 59, 141, 187
Presenting products and services in an appealing manner and raising money through sales, fund membership solicitation, and public relations
__Regulations Enforcement 163
Protecting the rights of individuals through enforcement of rules and policies involving finances, health, safety, immigration and customs
__Business Management 11, 31, 105, 115, 141, 191
Supervising all aspects of a business in such areas as lodging, recreation, amusement, transportation, services, and wholesale—retail

Contracts and Claims 87
Arranging contracts and setting claims with renters and leasers

PHYSICAL PERFORMING: Performing athletic skills before an audience
Sports 55, 173
Using athletic abilities to perform, coach, and officiate in sporting events

Appendix D–Personal Summary

Majors of Interest

Depending on your major and the college that you attend, you will take nearly one-half of your courses in subjects prescribed by that major. Typically, the coursework moves from introductory courses, becoming more complex, to higher level instruction.

Most colleges do not insist that you select a major before you enroll. Others require that you choose a major and list it on your application for admissions.

There are several advantages to selecting a major before you start on the big adventure—even if you are not entirely certain of your selection. First, you will receive information from your major about the program, what the courses and facilities are like, perhaps even some idea about your instructors. Second, you can read in the college catalog, or in the material sent from your major, suggestions for your first registration. This is especially important if you are in highly sequential programs like engineering, nursing, or business. If you do not make the right choices at the beginning, you may spend much of your time changing classes later on.

Look closely at the INTEREST AREAS WORK GROUPS, that you have checked and the indices to Courses, Majors, and Careers. Go to the pages indicated in *The Career Connection* and read about each major.

From information that you have gathered, what are 5 majors that interest you? List them in order of priority.

1. _____

2. _____

3. _____

4. _____

5. _____

Matching Majors to Jobs

There are two purposes for going to college. One is to increase your knowledge and appreciation for the artistic, scientific, and social aspects of the world around you. Another reason is to prepare for a career.

You will spend about 2,000 hours per year for 40 or more years working at your job. It will dictate the tasks you will perform each day, the money you will have available for expenses and desires, and the people with whom you will associate most of your waking hours. Perhaps most important of all, it will provide an opportunity for you to express yourself or to be of service to others.

By now you have noticed that there are several jobs associated with each major listed in *The Career Connection*. A national survey suggests that most graduates from these various majors enter jobs like the ones that are listed.

If you are looking for a major to help you get into a specific career, read the information on the majors you have selected and see if any of the jobs are of interest to you. List them in the space that follows. (Check the indices for an alphabetical listing of majors and careers.)

Majors	Jobs
1._____	_____
	_____
2._____	_____
	_____
3._____	_____
	_____
4._____	_____
	_____
5._____	_____
	_____

Choosing a Career

After reading over the job descriptions in the *Dictionary of Occupational Titles* or *The Enhanced Guide for Occupational Exploration,* answer the following questions for each of the jobs that you have selected and studied.

1. Will I be willing to get the education or training necessary for the job?

   _____

   _____

2. Will the job provide me with the income and benefits I desire?

   _____

   _____

3. How easy will it be for me to get into the occupations that I am considering?

   _____

   _____

4. Can I have the personal lifestyle I want if I pursue the job?

   _____

   _____

5. How happy will I be, week after week, performing the tasks and working in the environment associated with the job?

   _____

   _____

Appendix E–Taking the Next Steps

Having narrowed down some possibilities for a major and potential jobs, turn your attention to planning what your next moves should be.

Avoid the temptation of waiting until the last minute to act. There are definite payoffs for getting things done early.

You get the classes you want. Classes fill in a hurry; if you register late, you have to take the courses and faculty that are left.

Although not always the case, scholarships, grant-in-aid, and work-study programs are often limited and go to the first qualified applicants. If you get your financial package outlined and committed early, you can rest a little easier at night.

Here are some suggestions. Consider them, then add or delete as ideas come to you.

1. Select a college.

2. Check on the admission policies and procedures.

3. Consider the academic offerings to be sure it offers you what you are considering as a major.

4. Write to the academic advisement office for the course requirements for your potential majors.

5. Find out about costs and financial aids that may be available.

6. Check on housing if needed.

7. Make sure you know what courses are important to take for the first enrollment.

8. About two-thirds of the way through your first enrollment, make an appointment with your advisor to help you plan the remainder of your classes.

INDICES

INDEX OF COURSES

How well you like your high school courses predicts fairly well how well you will like similar courses in college. Most people also get their highest grades in technical courses similar to the high school courses where they have achieved well.

Following are courses categorized by content area. After each course are page numbers in *The Career Connection* that represent majors relating to the specific courses.

As you look over the courses, put a checkmark next to those in which you currently do well and enjoy. If you have not taken a course, but feel it is one that you would enjoy, check it also.

Social Science

Business 3 ,5, 31, 87, 115, 117, 187
Business Law 3, 29, 31, 85, 87
Civics 11, 69, 97, 109, 179, 199
Geography 9, 15, 19, 25, 33, 83, 97, 167
Government 9, 15, 25, 33, 69, 83, 109, 131, 133, 159, 179
History 9, 15, 25, 43, 69, 95, 109, 131, 133, 159, 171, 179
Psychology 67, 71,107, 117, 165, 183, 187, 197, 199, 215
Sociology 67, 117, 165, 183, 191, 197, 199

Mathematics

Applied Math 3, 29, 53, 85, 87
Algebra 143, 207
Geometry 7, 41, 61, 65, 143
Trigonometry 7, 37, 41, 53, 69, 73, 75, 101, 137, 139, 143, 145, 151, 155, 177, 207
Calculus 7, 41, 53, 69, 73, 75, 101, 137, 139, 143, 145, 151, 155, 177, 207
Computer Science 35, 53, 61, 65, 139, 143, 145

Fine Arts

Art 5, 21, 23, 47, 59, 61, 113, 129
Band 157
Choir 157
Drama 209
Graphics 5, 47, 59, 61, 65
Orchestra 157
Speech 49, 133, 209

INDEX OF MAJORS

Listed below are major areas of study along with the corresponding page numbers for more detailed information about that major.

INDEX OF MAJORS

INDEX OF CAREERS

The courses covered in this book are listed below, along with the page numbers where additional information can be found.

INDEX OF CAREERS

INDEX OF CAREERS

INDEX OF CAREERS

INDEX OF CAREERS

INDEX OF CAREERS

INDEX OF CAREERS

INDEX OF CAREERS

INDEX OF CAREERS

INDEX OF CAREERS

INDEX OF CAREERS

INDEX OF CAREERS

INDEX OF CAREERS

Other Titles
Available from
jist the job search people

Orders from individuals: Please use the form below (or provide the same information) to order additional copies of this or other books listed on this page. You are also welcome to send us your order (please enclose money order or check) or, if paying with a credit card, simply call our toll free number at **1-800-648-JIST** or **1-317-264-3720**. Our FAX number is **1-317-264-3709**. Qualified schools and organizations may request our catalog and obtain information on quantity discounts (we have over 400 career-related books, videos, software and other items). Our offices are open weekdays 8 a.m. to 5 p.m. local time and our address is:

JIST Works, Inc. • 720 North Park Avenue • Indianapolis, IN 46202-3431

QTY   TOTAL

_____ *The Career Connection: Guide to College Majors and Their Related Careers,*
Dr. Fred Rowe, $15.95   _____

_____ *The Career Connection II: Guide to Technical Majors and Their Related Careers,*
Dr. Fred Rowe, $13.95   _____

_____ *The Very Quick Job Search: Get a Good Job in Less Time,* J. Michael Farr, $9.95 _____

_____ *The Resume Solution: How to Write and Use a Resume That Gets Results,* David
Swanson, $10.95   _____

_____ *The Job Doctor: Good Advice on Getting a Good Job,* Dr. Phillip Norris, $8.95 _____

_____ *The Right Job for You: An Interactive Career Planning Guide,* J. Michael Farr,
$9.95

_____ *America's Top 300 Jobs: A Complete Career Handbook,* $17.95   _____

_____ *America's 50 Fastest Growing Jobs: An Authoritative Information Source,* $9.95 _____

_____ *America's Federal Jobs: A Complete Directory of Federal Career Opportunities,*
$14.95

_____ *Exploring Careers: A Young Person's Guide to over 300 Jobs,* $19.95   _____

_____ *Work in the New Economy: Careers and Job Seeking into the 21st Century,*
Robert Wegmann, $14.95   _____

_____ *The Occupational Outlook Handbook,* $16.95   _____

Subtotal _____

Sales Tax _____

(Shipping: $3 for first book, $1 for each addtional book.) Shipping _____

(U.S. Currency only) **TOTAL ENCLOSED WITH ORDER** _____

❑ **Check** ❑ **Money order**   ❑ **Credit Card:** ❑ **MasterCard** ❑ **VISA** ❑ **AMEX**
Card #_____Exp. Date_____

Name_____

Name of Organization (if applies) _____

Address _____

City/State/Zip _____

Daytime Telephone (   )_____-_____

Thank you for your order!